Brawdy

Brawdy

STRONGHOLD IN THE WEST

ALAN PHILLIPS

First published 2009

The History Press
The Mill, Brimscombe Port
Stroud, Gloucestershire, GL5 2QG
www.thehistorypress.co.uk

British Library Cataloguing in Publication Data.
A catalogue record for this book is available from the British Library.

ISBN 978 0 7524 4923 4

Typesetting and origination by The History Press
Printed in Great Britain

Contents

Introduction

Pembrokeshire has always been a military stronghold on the western edge of the British Isles and, especially at times of war, the county has attracted military planners. In the middle ages castles, and during the Napoleonic Wars forts, were built in prominent positions, taking advantage of the local geography.

Pembrokeshire, being a peninsular in a prominent position, became the ideal location for airfields in time of war. During the First World War planners saw the potential of the county in the fight against enemy submarines that were creating havoc with commercial shipping. Two bases were built: an airship and fighter-bomber base at Milton and a seaplane base at Fishguard Bay near the shipping port of Goodwick.

During the thirties the flying boat station at Pembroke Dock was constructed along with an airfield on the site of the Milton airship station, renamed RAF Carew. With the outbreak of war in 1939 there was an urgent need for airfields, and within two years several sites in the county were chosen.

By 1945 a total of fifteen bases and airfields of various description were built in the county: five were classed as active airfields, one a flying boat base, one a fighter station, while the others supported and trained coastal command air crews. The county was often referred as the world's largest aircraft carrier.

One of these airfields was Brawdy, situated on the west coast of Pembrokeshire, just off the A478, Haverfordwest to St David's road, the nearest village being Pen-y-Cwm. The airfield is situated on what can be described as a rugged yet beautiful coastline.

Not many airfields in the UK can claim to have been in control of the three services: the Royal Air Force, Royal Navy and the British Army.

Brawdy Airfield was built during the war, initially as a satellite airfield to RAF St David's, but as it turned out, the satellite proved a better-situated airfield than the former. RAF Brawdy was built in 1943 and became operational on 2 February 1944. It remained in RAF control until January 1946 when the airfield was handed over to the Admiralty for the Fleet Air Arm and became HMS Goldcrest. With the phasing out of the carriers and fixed wing aircraft the Admiralty return the airfield to the RAF.

RAF Brawdy was home to the No.1 Tactical Weapons Unit from 1974 to 1998 when the airfield closed. From 1998 the base was handed over to the Royal Corp of Signals and became known as Cawdor Barracks.

The author has called this book *Stronghold in the West*, which is translated from the Welsh motto 'Amddiffynfa y Gorllewin'. In a way the motto defines Brawdy Airfield's position in the UK, as Pembrokshire is one of the most westerly points in the country and therefore has always been ideally situated for the defence of the British Isles.

Acknowledgements

The author extends his gratitude to the following for their valuable assistance and information:

Aeroplane
Airfield Research Group
Air Pictorial
Arthur McEvoy
Aviation News
Benjamin Owen
British Aerospace Systems
Commander T L Jones RN (Rtd)
D. Edwards
DERA Aberporth
Doctor G. Middleton
Fleet Air Arm Museum, Yeovilton
Flight Magazine
Flight Lieutenant F.H. Spencer RAF (Rtd)
HMS Goldcrest, RNAS Brawdy
Haverfordwest Airport
Imperial War Museum, London and Manchester
J. James
Lieutenant Thomas J. Ritter, USN
Mike Bennett
Ministry of Defence

National Archives
Navy News
No.202 Squadron, Royal Air Force
Public Libraries – Haverfordwest and Fishguard
Public Records Office, Haverfordwest
RAF Brawdy
RAF Historical Branch
RAF Museum, Hendon
RAF News
Royal Corp of Signals
S/Ldr Ivor Griffiths
United States Navy
Welsh Assembly Government Photographic Archives
Western Mail
Western Telegraph

I would also like to thank numerous individuals who have contributed a wealth of information and photographs for this book, and extend a special thanks to all the ex-servicemen and women of both the Royal Air Force and the Royal Navy, whose generous assistance has made this book possible.

Chapter 1

Brawdy Airfield Location

It is very rare in military history that an airfield has control of all three military services, but that is what happened to the airfield at Brawdy in Pembrokeshire.

Brawdy opened during the Second World War as a Royal Air Force base. Then, after the war, was taken over by the Admiralty for the Royal Navy Fleet Air Arm, and then reverted back to RAF ownership, before eventually becoming an army camp.

When war was declared on 3 September 1939 there were only fifteen military airfields in the UK, with only two in Pembrokeshire: the flying boat station at Pembroke Dock, which opened on 1 January 1930, and the support airfield at Carew Cheriton, opened in 1937. During the early war years there was a great urgency to build new airfields, and by 1945 a further 444 airfields had been constructed in the UK.

In Wales thirty-nine military airfields of various descriptions were built, some flying boat stations, others satellite airfields, relief landing grounds and aircraft factories with concrete runways and grass landing grounds.

The events leading to the outbreak of hostilities in 1939 resulted in the earmarking of several sites in Wales for airfield development, a programme which proceeded rapidly once war was declared. It is worth noting that several of the original sites chosen were surveyed by Sir Alan Cobham in the twenties.

There were two main fighter stations: RAF Valley, in Anglesey, and Fairwood Common, on the Gower Peninsular, with a number of subsidiaries at Angle, Llanbedr, Pembrey and Wrexham. Most of the airfields and bases in Pembrokeshire played a significant role in the Battle of the Atlantic under the control of No. 19 Group RAF Coastal Command. The bulk of the other airfields and bases were involved in personnel training, air gunnery, bomb aiming and providing target facilities, except for Broughton

The site in 1941 of where Brawdy Airfield would eventually be built. (Welsh Assembly Government)

The approach to the airfield over Newgale Beach. (Via Dr G. Middleton)

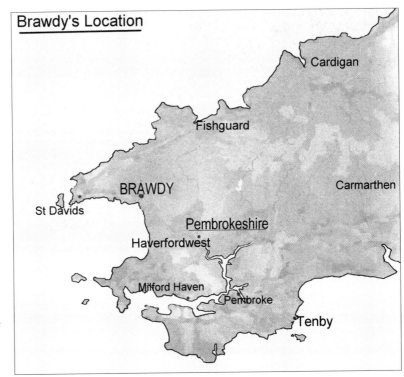

Map of Pembrokeshire showing Brawdy's location.

and Beaumaris which were involved in aircraft building, providing maintenance units and storage space at Llandow and St Athan.

As a result of the outbreak of hostilities seven airfields plus a storage unit were built in Pembrokeshire, adding to the bases that already existed.

A detailed air and ground survey was conducted during 1937/38 for possible airfield sites in the county. The possible sites were of fairly flat terrain with an all-round visibility, while probable sites required a great deal of construction work, including levelling. According to some sources a total of over twenty sites were considered for airfield construction.

The Brawdy and St David's site was surveyed in detail in early 1941 as possible sites for land-based aircraft in the fight against the U-boat menace. Work did not begin on St David's until 1942, as up to then priority was given to the construction of fighter airfields.

Brawdy Airfield, as already mentioned, is situated on the west coast of Pembrokeshire, just off the Haverfordwest to St David's road (A478). One naval rating who was brought up in a city remarked that he never knew such beauty existed until he was posted to Brawdy. Admittedly the coastline is of remarkable beauty, like it has been painted by a master artist, but in winter it can be completely different, with chilling winds blowing in from the Atlantic.

Perhaps the worst winter experienced by Brawdy's personnel was in 1947 when most of Pembrokeshire was hit by freezing and heavy snowfalls which cut off villages and remote areas for weeks. All the roads, including the coast road, were completely blocked. As soon as sections were re-opened by local authority workers snowdrifts closed them off again, often within hours. So the airfield was cut off from the outside for about ten days and, because of the high winds and snow storms, no flying was possible. The station had only sufficient rations for about two days, three at the most.

As Brawdy was situated near the coast the Admiralty ordered the destroyer HMS *Roebuck* to St Brides Bay from Milford Haven with supplies. The warship anchored just offshore with supplies being ferried by a landing craft to the small rocky beach of Cwm Bach, and then carried by sailors both from Brawdy and from the warship up the difficult cliff face to be loaded onto trucks. Fortunately the road cleared that morning had not become re-blocked by snow. Nevertheless, as a result the Admiralty decreed that in future all naval air stations and other naval establishments have sufficient emergency rations to last five days or more.

Throughout the airfield's redevelopment post Second World War the Ministry of Defence has worked closely with the council and the Pembrokeshire National Park to minimise as much as possible this blot on the landscape. This is evidently so when travelling on the Haverfordwest to St David's road as the majority of the buildings, with the exception of some hangars, are built in a dip in the contour of the land and therefore cannot be seen from the main road.

The camp at Brawdy both under the Admiralty and the Royal Air Force has always regarded itself as part of the county. It has integrated itself as a small town between Newgale and St David's.

Personnel from the airfield were always involved with the community and provided support for activities in the county. The various commanding officers were always available to attend the various local functions, whether it was an official dinner in the town hall in Haverfordwest or opening a summer fête or flower show in Letterston or Mathry. Schools in the county also benefit from the military presence at Brawdy, with school children having an opportunity to visit the airfield as guests of the services. And, of course, HMS Goldcrest, RAF Brawdy and Cawdor Barracks have always provided personnel for the annual Remembrance Day parades, which are appreciated by the veterans.

Sports were another aspect of integration. All three services are keen for their servicemen to partake in sports events. Both the Navy and the RAF had their own soccer, rugby and cricket teams, which contributed to the various local leagues. Today 14 Signal Regiment has kept up this close relationship with the county by entering soccer and rugby teams into the local leagues.

If at any time in the future the Ministry of Defence decides to close Brawdy, it will not be just a military base that it will be closing but a little town overlooking St Brides Bay.

Chapter 2

Airfield Development

Plans for an airfield at Brawdy were drawn up in 1941 when the site was photographed from the air by the RAF, but work did not begin until the end of 1942. Within a matter of months farmland with neat fields had been levelled and drains had been laid. The heavy earth levelling equipment was transferred from nearby St David's Airfield, and by the end of the year the site was ready for the foundations of the three runways. Initial plans for the airfield included the standard wartime 'A' in its runway configuration, like St David's, but, due to the terrain and the prevailing winds that blew in from the sea, the layout was modified.

Brawdy runways were constructed so that all three crossed each other on the eastern side, taking advantage of the prevailing winds, enabling aircraft to take off fully loaded. This was in complete contrast to the triangular pattern of St David's, which suffered severe problems from winds blowing in various directions. As a consequence, aircraft were not able to operate fully loaded from the airfield. The procedure, therefore, would be to 'bomb up' at St David's with a light enough fuel load for the take off, then land at Brawdy to fill their tanks and proceed on their anti-submarine/surface ship patrols, which was unsatisfactory. Landing with a bomb bay full of ordinance is not a favourable procedure by any crew.

Throughout 1943 building proceeded at a fast pace: runway 03/21 was 2,000 yards, 08/26 1,420 yards, and 15/33 1,990 yards, together with a perimeter and thirty looped/spectacle/diamond hard standings in five clusters. The watch tower was the standard 1941 pattern commonly used on bomber satellite stations. However, it was upgraded in 1945 to the 1943 pattern control tower. Most of the administration, the various messes, sick quarters and accommodation quarters were either Nissen, Maycrete or wooden buildings. The Nissen hut was the most common type built on airfields in 1942/43 as

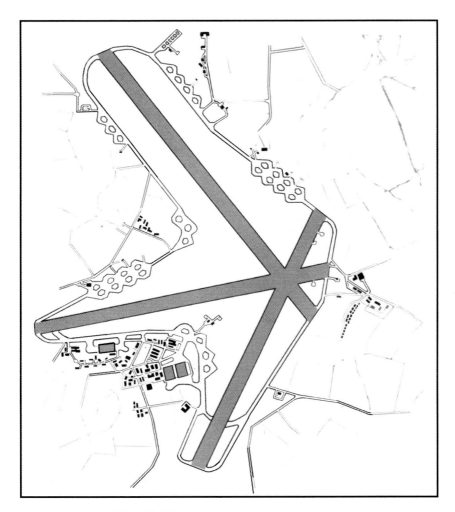

Layout drawing of the airfield in 1945.

they were easily constructed, requiring less man hours, and were half the cost of the Maycrete huts or brick buildings.

Only one T2 type hangar was available when the airfield opened, but another two were added when the headquarters moved from St David's in 1945. The T2 hangar was mostly earmarked for bomber or bomber Operational Conversion Unit (OCU) airfields, as their span was larger than the Bellman hangars which were used on fighter and training airfields.

A bomb and explosive dump was constructed on the north-eastern corner of the airfield, near heading 15°, on runway 15/33. It was constructed to the standard ministry plans of separate concrete pans protected by earth embankments.

The main entrance to the camp was just off the A478, with four secondary and emergency entrances around the perimeter track leading from small unclassified country roads. Most of the accommodation blocks were situated on the road leading to the airfield.

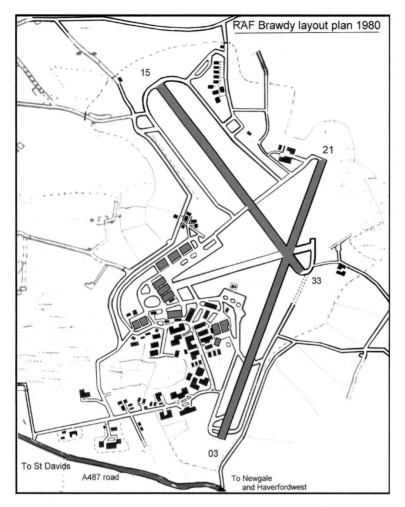

15

21

33

03

To St Davids

A487 road

To Newgale
and Haverfordwest

Layout drawing of the airfield in 1980.

Brawdy runways were constructed so that all three runways crossed each other to
take advantage of the prevailing winds. This was completely different to the standard
war time triangular pattern previously used at St David's, which suffered severely from
changing wind directions. Whenever possible crew preferred to take off and land at
Brawdy rather than at their home station.

RAF Brawdy became operational on 2 February 1944 as a satellite to St David's,
about seven miles away. Both airfields were under the control of No. 19 Group RAF
Coastal Command.

Coastal Command found the airfield at St David's unsatisfactory for its operations as
too many unnecessary landing mishaps occurred. So on 1 November 1945 the station
headquarters and its resident squadrons and units transferred to RAF Brawdy, leaving
the former base as the satellite airfield. New T2 hangars had already been built at
Brawdy to accommodate the in-coming squadrons.

Brawdy control tower during Royal Navy control.

When the RAF took control of the airfield several modifications were carried out on the control tower.

Aerial view of Brawdy
taken in 1990. (Welsh
Assembly Government)

Several of St David's Airfield buildings, in particular the Maycrete and Nissen huts, were demolished and rebuilt at Brawdy.

When No. 517 Squadron left on 30 November 1945 the only aircraft remaining were Avro Ansons, Tiger Moths and Chipmunks belonging to the station flight. Within a month most of the station administration, sick quarters and other staff had left, leaving a skeleton staff for care and maintenance.

Royal Navy Presence

Brawdy Airfield only remained idle for a brief period, as on 1 January 1946 it was officially transferred to Admiralty control as a naval air station.

The Royal Navy was short of large airfields with reasonable length runways, especially for their twin-engine aircraft used for training. Most of the Admiralty airfields at the

In 1995 30 per cent of the airfield structures were demolished including the crew room of D Flight No.202 SAR squadron. (Via Dr Middleton)

Brawdy's remaining hangars in 2007.

Three T2 hangars from St David's rebuilt at Brawdy.

time were used mainly for the use of carrier-based aircraft while the carriers were in dock or being modernised. Brawdy was commissioned HMS Goldcrest II, a Relief Landing Ground (RLG), or in naval terms a 'tender airfield' for Goldcrest I, which was Royal Naval Air Station Dale, another former RAF airfield.

When the RAF left Brawdy most of the airfield equipment like the fire tenders, refuelling tankers, tractors and the airfield control were left behind. Even the catering installation, sick quarters and some office and accommodation furnishings were in place for the new owners.

Initially, Admiralty personnel was limited to a skeleton staff for overseeing fire and rescue services, refuelling, security, aircraft controllers and, eventually, from December 1946, personnel from No.811 squadron. HMS Goldcrest I at Dale provided any additional staff or equipment needed.

Few alterations were carried out during this period, as the Admiralty was not certain whether the airfield was suitable for their operations.

For the next eighteen months the airfield was fairly busy, used by its resident aircraft as well as aircraft from No.748 squadron, based at the naval night fighting school at Dale.

With cessation of hostilities there was a general run-down in flying training in the three services and, in particular, the Fleet Air Arm. No.748 squadron at Dale was disbanded on 10 September 1946, and therefore the importance of the night fighting school diminished, which left the future of the tender airfield at Brawdy in doubt.

On 30 September 1947 the Admiralty put the airfield on care and maintenance, at six months notice of service, although earlier in the year plans had been drawn up to keep Brawdy open as a naval air station with the prospect of extensive modernisation.

In a very short period the airfield deteriorated, runways and perimeter tracks started to break up, buildings leaked and were no longer fit for habitation and the approach and landing lights were in need of replacing. The list was endless. And, to make the situation worse, several of the Nissen huts were either blown down or completely lost their galvanised cladding in high winds over the years.

Work began on the extensive modernisation programme in early 1951, and for the next five years the airfield became a large building site. The actual modernisation took longer than the time taken to build the airfield in 1943/44. All the runways were resurfaced, but only 03/21 was lengthened by 500ft. Runway headings were as follows: 03/21 6,022ft × 150ft, 08/26 4,267ft × 150ft and 15/33 6,031ft × 150ft. On the runways there were a total of 488 thirty-watt lights for illumination, together with obstruction lights on Roch Castle operated from the control tower. The taxiways and the diamond hard standings were also resurfaced and modified. New runway approach lighting was installed, as well as full airfield flood lighting covering the aprons, some of the taxiing area and hard standings. The wartime control tower was more or less completely rebuilt; modified to Admiralty standard by adding a completely new glassed viewing section and a glass house on the roof. It was also fitted with the most up to date radio receivers and transmission equipment available.

It was not just the airfield that was modernised but also the accommodation and administration areas. New central heating brick quarters and dining halls for senior and junior ranks were built. New Maycrete and Nissen huts were built on the approach to the main gate for visiting personnel, providing spare accommodation if needed. Several married quarters were built near the entrance to the station, mostly for the senior ranks, while over 100 two- and three-bedroom houses for the junior ranks were built just off the Broad Haven Road in Haverfordwest.

RNAS Brawdy was declared fully operational in 1956, although it had continued to function throughout the building programme.

Hangar space at Brawdy was limited to three T2 hangars, so when the Fleet Requirement Unit returned to Brawdy in October 1958, St David's three T-hangars were surplus to requirement. In early 1959 the hangars were moved and constructed at Brawdy, adding valuable hangar space. The three hangars were built on the diamond hard standing to the north of the east/west runway (08/26).

T2 type hangars were the hallmark of bomber and conversion unit airfields. They were easily assembled and transportable. The hangars were found to be suitable for aircraft overhaul as they had a greater roof clearance than most types and were capable of having an overhead hoist. Brawdy and St David's hangars were 1942 types, which were 37ft in height, 113ft in width and 240ft in length.

During the re-building programme in the early sixties six more Admiralty type hangars were built (3 × Mainhill and 3 × Mains hangars). Three of the new hangars were constructed at the end of the east/west runway, and were used by the Naval Aircraft support unit. These were unique because they were interconnecting with an adjoining technical block. The hangars were used for storing 'moth-balled' aircraft in a humidity-free environment. East/west runway became an additional parking and servicing apron.

The Mains and Mainhill hangars were mostly used by the Admiralty and were also transportable. These hangars were smaller than the T2 with a span of 60ft and a door width of 55ft, a height of 17–20ft and a length of 84–105ft.

In 1958 Brawdy's future was in doubt, even after millions of pounds had been spent on modernising the base. The Admiralty put forward plans to consolidate the Fleet Air Arm fixed wing element at just three locations. Brawdy was not included in this initial plan. However, after a consultation period the plan was revised and Brawdy was saved and given the additional new role of advance training.

Further modernisation then took place: runways were lengthened, new taxiways were built while old ones were broken up and a new apron was added between the tower and hangars, in place of the hard standings. The control tower equipment was brought up to RAF standard and new radar was installed on the airfield.

Runway 03/21 was extended once again, this time by 1,500ft, making it capable of handling most military aircraft in service. New accommodation was built especially for the WRENS due to be posted to the base. Additional houses were built at the naval estate at Haverfordwest.

After all of this extensive modernisation, flying resumed on 1 August 1963.

Following a Government decision to phase out the Fleet Air Arm fixed wing element as the result of decommissioning the navy's aircraft carriers in 1968, the Admiralty had no further need for RNAS Brawdy and the tenure was relinquished on 1 April 1971, the last FAA flight taking place on 1 December 1970.

From 1971 to 1974 the airfield came under the control of the Department of Environment, whose civilian team kept the base fully maintained and in reasonable order. It was important that the heating boilers were properly maintained to provide hot water for the central heating system, making sure that all buildings were kept dry and ready for use.

The Admiralty removed all naval equipment and vehicles during 1971, although the stored aircraft were removed at a later date.

There was great concern in the county over the closure of the airfield as its presence contributed to the finance of the county in commerce, and was a source of local employment. It would not only be the towns of Haverfordwest and St David's that would suffer but also the villages located near the airfield that relied on the base personnel using their amenities and shops, as well as local producers who supplied the meat, vegetables, milk and daily newspapers.

As a result of another defence review it was decided that the Royal Air Force would use the airfield, but at the time its specific role was not finalised. However, one thing was certain: with the departure of the FAA search and rescue helicopters, Pembrokeshire lost its air rescue service.

On 1 January 1971 the RAF took control of the airfield, and within a month 'D' Flight of No.22 squadron took up residence with two Westland Whirlwind HAR 10s. Initially there were only modest changes to the airfield, mainly the installation of RAF radio equipment. As the RAF tenure proceeded further, changes and major building work took place. Modifications were carried out on the Admiralty Mains and Mainhill hangars, the wartime T2 hangars were reroofed and the control tower was updated to RAF standards, to become a vertical split-level type.

Before the decade was over two of the runways were resurfaced and reinforced making them capable of handling the heaviest aircraft. The three inter-connecting hangars were used for storage and maintenance while the remaining hangars were allocated to different squadrons.

As Brawdy had been designated a forward fighter base, with Hawks in a secondary fighter defence role, it was planned to construct six hardened aircraft shelters on either side of runway 15/33 during the 1980 modernisation programme. However, because of costs, and because HARs were more urgently needed on frontline operational airfields, the plan was shelved, although several hard standing pads were allocated to Phantoms and fitted with their own starting units for quick response.

In 1992 the Ministry of Defence announced that jet-flying training would cease at Brawdy and the resident No. 1 tactical weapons unit would be disbanded.

The last training flight took place on 28 August 1992, and before the end of the year both Squadron Nos 79 and 234 had also been disbanded and their Hawk aircraft allocated to other units or put in storage.

The only unit left at Brawdy was 'B' Flight of No. 202 Search and Rescue Squadron, which remained at the airfield until the end of the summer.

Throughout the rest of the year after the personnel had left, contractors moved in to remove all remaining RAF equipment.

For a short period the airfield was put on care and maintenance but, due to the fall of the Soviet block countries and the withdrawal of British troops from West Germany, there was an acute shortage of bases for these units. Throughout the UK several redundant RAF airfields were allocated. So, in January 1996, Brawdy became the base for the 14 Signal Regiment, Royal Corp of Signals, and the camp known as Cawdor Barracks.

Only a small part of the 800-acre site was required by the Signal Regiment. A total of £9 million was spent by the Ministry of Defence to bring the camp up to modern standards. David Mclean Group was awarded the contract, and work began in December 1995, being completed a year later. New married quarters were also built at Cashfield Farm, Crowhill, Haverfordwest. Most of the money was spent on the refurbishment of the barrack blocks, administration offices and the conversion of four blocks for female accommodation. A 4km, 2.4m-high fence was built around the accommodation blocks and other sensitive areas of the camp. Most of the fence was put up below horizon level so as not to spoil the surrounding area.

A new operation block was equipped with modern electronic devices such as an indoor firing range capable of utilising the latest laser range finders.

Some of the hangars were repainted and refurbished, as the regiment utilised them for vehicle and equipment storage, maintenance and indoor training. Three of the older hangars were demolished in 1997/98 and sold.

The large apron and hard standing lighting towers that dominated the airfield skyline, built at a considerable cost in the early nineties, were removed.

Therefore, the runways were no longer required, and, at the time of writing, have been broken up, only being used by the Brawdy Motor Club for straight-line racing.

Since the arrival of the army several of the airfield's buildings have been demolished, including the control tower which was demolished in a training exercise with the Special Air Service in 1996.

Towards the end of 1995 and throughout the rebuilding phase, 30 per cent of the airfield structures were demolished.

In 1973 the United States Navy built a base just off the road leading to the airfield, which was officially known as an Oceanographic Research Station. It was situated well away from the airfield's operational side, and its existence was often denied. Whenever an article appeared in the newspapers the editor was threatened with the Official Secrets Act.

Years after it was closed, and long after the fall of the Soviet block countries, information was released. The base was a processing centre for a network of underwater microphones, submerged off the British coast and well into the Atlantic, listening to submarine movements (mostly Soviet).

It was known as the Sound Surveillance System, or SOSUS. Project Caesar, as it was referred to in documents, comprised several bases capable of tracking all Soviet submarine movements between their home bases and the Atlantic. Brawdy was the main base in Europe and its structures were built to house the most sophisticated equipment available. All the buildings were humidity free and kept at a certain temperature. The base was self-sufficient with its own generators and boiler house.

The officers and senior non-commission officers were put in their respective RAF messes, while the ratings had their own accommodation block among the junior ranks.

With the prospect of the airfield closing, the USN closed the base on 1 October 1995 and its functions were transferred to a new establishment at RAF St Mawgan in Cornwall. The sensitive equipment was flown out in USAF Lockheed Galaxy transport aircraft, which at the time were the heaviest aircraft to land in Pembrokeshire.

Chapter 3

The RAF Period
1944–1946

RAF Brawdy was built as a satellite airfield for St David's, under the control of No.19 Group RAF Coastal Command. The airfield was officially opened on 2 February 1944. Most of the airfield's movements were by aircraft from the parent station, landing at Brawdy to be fully loaded for their patrol missions, because of the crosswind problems at the parent airfield. Aircraft involved in this arrangement were Handley Page Halifax bombers of Nos 58, 502 and 517 Squadrons. The first squadron to leave was No.58 in August 1944, which departed for Stornaway, followed in September by No.502 Squadron.

From February 1944 both Nos 58 and 502 Squadrons operated from both St David's and Brawdy, as the airfield had become the squadron's second base. It was during this arrangement that the squadrons recorded several outstanding successes.

On 17 March 1944, after the usual 'topping up' at Brawdy, while on patrol F/O Galbraith sighted two surface vessels and dropped 2,000lb of bomb on the targets. One vessel was left ablaze while the other was beginning to burn. When another aircraft returned to the scene one of the ships had sank and the crew had abandoned the other.

Later F/O Galbraith was awarded the Distinguished Flying Cross (DFC) and the George Medal (GM) for his exploits with No.502 while based in West Wales. The GM was awarded for his airmanship when, after being attacked by seven Ju88s, with one of his air gunners killed and another crew member wounded, he outflew the enemy aircraft, returning home to the base and landing safely. It is worth noting that others of his crew were also decorated. Flt Sgt Forbes, the flight engineer, was awarded the DFM and GM, and 1st Lieutenant C.D. Kramer USAAF, on loan to Coastal Command, received the American Medal for Bravery.

On 25 April 1944 Canadian Flt Lt Holderness AFC sank an enemy submarine in what was a classic Coastal Command Halifax night attack. After hours of patient patrolling, usually without any contact, during which time boredom is the greater enemy, a blip appeared on the radar screen. The aircraft circled the location and dropped some flares, illuminating a surfaced U-boat. Within minutes the Halifax dived with its bomb doors opened, dropping bombs and depth charges on the target. Most of the bombs just straddled the submarine, but one found its mark and the submarine was cut in half. The Halifax returned safely to St David's with only a 37mm cannon hole in its wing.

In a small ceremony at Brawdy on 24 May 1944 Squadron Leader C.A. Maton was promoted to commanding officer of No.502 Squadron, with the rank of wing commander. This was a real landmark in Coastal Command history, for a rear gunner to hold the title of squadron CO.

Since the invasion of the Channel Islands, the island ports had been a haven for U-boats sheltering, refuelling and acquiring provisions. Nos 58 and 502 found the area rich pickings for submarines. On 3 June a U-boat was attacked and badly damaged in Guernsey Harbour. On the nights of 5 and 6 June 1944, during the initial D-Day landings at Normandy, No.502 Squadron operated anti-U-boat and enemy shipping patrols from Brawdy to the English Channel, with at least two U-boat hits claimed. As the result of squadron efforts and achievements, two of the personnel were awarded the DFC and nine were mentioned in despatches in the half-yearly honours.

Handley Page Halifax GR2 of No.58 Squadron.

Crew of a Halifax of No.58 Squadron after a patrol in the Bay of Biscay.

Mishaps were common at St David's. This HP Halifax (XX177) of No. 517 Squadron broke in two during a crash landing. (Via RAF Brawdy)

On 8 June 1944 a St David's based Halifax 'F' (for Freddie) of No. 502 Squadron, captained by Flying Officer J. Spurgeon, took off from Brawdy with a full load of fuel and ordnance, for a long patrol. An hour into this patrol, at about 0145 a.m., he sighted and attacked U-413. The aircraft made a run in on the target with its front .303 guns firing. Despite accurate heavy flak coming from the submarine, he managed to drop four 600lb anti-submarine bombs. Three of the bombs missed the target, but the fourth seriously damaged the conning tower. Sensing a kill, the Halifax made four more machine-gun attacks on the submarine, and on the fifth received a direct hit to its port engine and had to break off the engagement. Due to substantial damage the Halifax was unable to return to Brawdy, so F/O Spurgeon decided to make for RAF Predannack where he landed safely, while the U-boat slithered back to a French port and was out of action for some time.

Throughout the next few months the two squadrons were extremely busy. Four enemy submarines were attacked and sunk, and seven surface targets, including a German destroyer off the north-west coast of France, were destroyed.

Again, on 20 June 1944, the Channel Islands ports became a target when No. 502 Squadron commanding officer, Wing Commander Morton, led a low-level raid on U-boats sheltering in St Peter's Port, Guernsey. Then, on 23 June, Halifax 'T' (for Tommy) of No. 58 Squadron sank an enemy submarine in Alderney Harbour.

In the post D-Day period both Nos 58 and 502 Squadrons' Halifaxs were reverted back to their bomber role when they were involved in 'ranger' patrols over mainland

HP Halifax GR2 (J for Johnnie) of No. 502 Squadron over the Pembrokeshire countryside.

A Halifax GR3 of No. 502 Squadron landing with its wheels up at Brawdy.

Crew of a Halifax Met V of No. 517 Squadron about to undertake a dusk patrol. (Flt Lt G. Jones)

HP Halifax Met V of No. 517 Squadron.

De Havilland Mosquitoes PR IV of No.8 OTU being serviced at Brawdy. Some of the aircraft had shrouded exhausts similar to the night fighters. (B. Owen)

A Supermarine Spitfire PR XI of No.8 OTU.

Europe. The purpose of the patrols were to try and stop enemy reinforcements from reaching the beachhead at Normandy, which basically involved bombing and strafing any troop, armour and supply movements.

Also there were tragedies: several aircraft were lost along with their crews.

As the Allied armies advanced through Europe, Coastal Command decided to reduce the number of airfields in the UK, especially those specialising in anti-shipping and anti-submarine operations, concentrating more on the bases on the south coast of England and the flying boat stations. Therefore, the importance of St David's, and eventually Brawdy, diminished.

With the departure of No. 58 Squadron, in August 1944, for Stornaway, and No. 502, in September, St David's Airfield was diminished and Brawdy became the active airfield.

The first RAF squadron to be based at Brawdy was No. 517, which moved from St David's on 2/3 February. No. 517 was equipped with the four-engine Handley Page Halifax Mk II and Mk V bombers, which were modified for meteorological duties as Met 3 and Met 5, covering the western approaches. The Halifax was ideally suited to the task as it could carry various kinds of equipment and a sizeable fuel load, which gave it up to ten hours' airtime.

The meteorological data obtained by the squadron from their long-range patrols over the Atlantic Ocean and the Bay of Biscay was invaluable to military planning, because, during the war, there were no such things as weather ships patrolling in the Atlantic, where most of the British weather comes from.

The Met aircraft would fly at different altitudes to gather barometer readings and temperature, so the data could be analysed by meteorologists in the UK who could then plot approaching weather fronts due to come over the British Isles and Europe. Had it not been for this weather information gathering the D-Day landings at Normandy would not have been possible. Throughout the invasion its planners received continuous up to date weather data.

The aircraft had proved their reliability and toughness while operating patrol duties with Nos 58 and 502 Squadrons.

The Handley Page Halifax Mk II, V, GR2 and Met IIIs were all powered by four Rolls Royce Merlin XX engines of 1,390hp each, giving an average speed of 265mph and, with an extra fuel tank in the bomb bay, a range of nearly 2,000 miles.

No. 517 Squadron was formed at St Eval as No. 1404 MET Flight, but was renumbered No. 517 on 11 August 1943 and allocated an establishment of eighteen aircraft, plus six in reserve, of the Met III, Met V and VI versions of the Halifax. The squadron's other equipment included Hampdens, Hudsons, Fortresses and a Short Stirling Met 4s, used for meteorological training. When the squadron moved to Brawdy on 2 February 1944 it was allocated 'epicure' patrols in the Atlantic and the Bay of Biscay.

In March 1945 No. 517 Squadron began converting to Halifax Met Mk IIIs, Vs and VIs, which it operated until March 1946.

The squadron remained at Brawdy until September 1945, when it moved to Weston Zoyland, although the squadron's Halifaxs made the occasional landing at Brawdy when returning from patrols. The squadron was disbanded at RAF Chivenor in June 1946 and its aircraft transferred to its sister Met squadron, No. 518 (MET).

The squadron losses were mostly due to bad weather and mechanical problems rather than enemy action. The Luftwaffe also used aircraft to gather weather information and several of their anti-shipping aircraft, Focke Wulf FW200 Condors, were converted for the task. According to some sources, although the RAF denies it, there was an understanding between aircrews that neither side would interfere with each other in the event of an encounter. Nevertheless, pilots and gun crews were always on alert.

Despite its functions the squadron was not immune to the problems brought about by the elements (and the occasional mechanical problem), and on several occasions aircraft were diverted as far as Gibraltar or to bases in North Africa.

No.517 Squadron was not regarded as a front line operational squadron like Nos 58 and 502, but on a number of occasions it was involved in skirmishes with enemy aircraft while on weather patrols, when the mutual understanding between the aircrews was ignored.

However, bad weather and mechanical problems took their toll on the squadron. One event took place in June 1944, when a Halifax LL144, code X9 F (for Freddie), piloted by F/O Aveling, a Canadian serving in the RAF, was on a weather-gathering mission in connection with the D-Day operations. Well into his mission, some 800 miles from the Pembrokeshire coast, the aircraft developed mechanical and engine failure. After considering the situation they were in, with no hope of returning to Brawdy, or any other airfield for that matter, they decided to ditch the Halifax in the Atlantic. With great skill F/O Aveling ditched the aircraft in rough seas, and the crew were able to climb into their dinghies. After three days adrift the crew was eventually picked up by an American ship and taken to the United States. However, other crews were not so fortunate. The crew of Halifax LK962 crashed into the Atlantic on 14 November 1944 with no sign of survivors. The reason for the crash is still unknown, but it is believed that it was due to mechanical failure rather than enemy action.

Within days of opening RAF Brawdy a large force of Ju88s attacked the surrounding area. Fortunately the raiders were intercepted and shot down over St Bride's Bay by fighters based at Fairwood. A returning Halifax was caught up in the fight and, presumably, shot down. Only a single main wheel was ever found. Another Halifax low on fuel managed to dodge the combat area and was able to reach the airfield in safety.

By October 1944 service personnel based at Brawdy numbered eighty RAF and one WAAF officer, as well as 1,320 other ranks, of which 185 were WAAF. This figure remained more or less the same until July 1945.

In early 1945 Withybush Airfield, near Haverfordwest, had severe parking problems, so a detachment of thirty Spitfires and Mosquitoes of No.8 Operational Training Unit became a lodger unit at Brawdy on 27 February. They remained there until June 1945 when all eight OTU left the county for their new base at Mount Farm. The unit was responsible for training photoreconnaissance personnel for the RAF.

Like all training units No.8 OTU had its share of mishaps. On 20 February 1945, while on a reconnaissance exercise over Snowdonia, Mosquito NT221 made a forced landing on the beach at Harlech due to an engine fire. Initially the landing went according to plan, but the aircraft was unable to stop on the wet sand and hit a sand dune. The crew managed to get out of the aircraft before it was engulfed in flames, but the pilot sustained head and chest injuries on landing and had to be helped out of the aircraft. The crew was taken to RAF Llandwrog, but the pilot died from his injuries.

Fortunately some other mishaps had a happier conclusion. On 16 May 1945 three Spitfires and one Mosquito took off on a photo-reconnaissance flight over the coast of South Wales and the Severn Estuary. The training flight long overdue, an alert was sent out to other airfields while two Mosquitoes and an Anson despatched from Brawdy to search for the missing aircraft. Eventually the flight was traced to Withybush, as the aircraft had returned there by mistake. No one thought of informing the Brawdy operation room!

On 7 February 1945 three Martinets and two Spitfire XIIs of No. 595 Squadron based at Aberporth were detached to Brawdy for three weeks, as this was the nearest station to the anti-aircraft school at Manorbier. After carrying out target towing sorties, they returned to Aberporth on the last day of February. A further detachment of Spitfire VB and XIIs of No. 595 Squadron from Aberporth arrived on 27 February and remained until June. The detachment was involved in trials with target gliders, providing practice for the coastal AA batteries.

These TG Mk I target gliders were built by the FROG Company. They had a 16ft wingspan and were fitted with a skid undercarriage, and, at the time, were an improvement on the standard target tows. It is a strange irony that during Brawdy's early days the airfield was earmarked as a base for pilotless aircraft, but the idea was shelved.

The HQ was officially moved from St David's to Brawdy on 1 November 1945 and the former airfield was designated a satellite landing ground, although most of the squadron's personnel were based at Brawdy months earlier.

It is also worth noting that in June 1945 Liberator VI and VIIIs of Nos 53 and 220 Squadrons, which had been transferred to RAF Transport Command, were based at St David's and used Brawdy as a relief airfield.

No. 53 Squadron was transferred from Reykjavik in Iceland equipped with twenty-one Consolidated Liberators (sixteen Mk VIs and five Mk VIIIs) under the command of Wing Commander D. Mckenzie, while No. 220 Squadron, with fifteen Liberator Mk VI and VIIs, was posted from the Azores under the command of Wing Commander B.O. Diaz DFC.

As the RAF had a shortage of long-range transport aircraft several Liberators were converted to the role. All armaments, including the bomb bay, were removed to accommodate extra passengers. These aircraft were seen on a number of occasions at Brawdy. One eyewitness reported seeing at least ten Liberators parked on the hard standings at eastern end of the airfield. Both squadrons left Wales on 17 September 1945 to fulfil trooping duties in India, where they remained until being disbanded on 25 May 1946.

Tragically not all the aircrews made it this far. While on a night training exercise Liberator Mk VIII (KH183) crashed some two miles from St David's Airfield, after taking off in June 1943, in a field belonging to Emlych Farm between the town of St David's and Whitesand Bay. This was not far from the site where a USAAF Martin Marauder bomber would later crash, in Carn LLiddi near Porth Mawr. Flight

Lieutenant Charles Grayson, Flight Lieutenant Thomas Hugh Topping, Flying Officer William George Mills and Flight Sergeant Peter Newton Scott were killed.

Two of the aircrew, Flt Lt Topping and F/O Mills, are buried at City Road Cemetery, Haverfordwest, while Flt Lt Grayson is buried at Lewes, Sussex, and Flt Sgt Scott at Sleaford Cemetery in Lincoln.

Today a memorial plaque stands at Emlych Farm on the site the tragedy took place in July 1945. The unveiling of the plaque service took place in July 1995, and was attended by the Dean of St David's, the Very Reverend J. Wyn Evans, the commanding officer of RAF Brawdy, Squadron Leader D. Warneford, Mrs A. Flude of Hayscastle, niece of Flt Lt Grayson, Mrs C. Rees and Miss M. Rees of Emlych Farm. Also present were members of the Pembrokeshire Aviation Group, who co-ordinated the service.

Ironically, most of the squadron was due to be located at Brawdy later in the month. Both Nos 53 and 220 Squadrons were officially based at St David's, but, like the Halifax crews before them, they preferred flying from Brawdy Airfield.

Despite the crash the squadrons continued flying training and familiarisation operations, until No. 53 Squadron moved to RAF Merryfield and No. 220 to RAF Waterbeach, in September, en route to the Far East.

With the end of hostilities in Europe the need for military airfields diminished, so the writing was on the walls in Brawdy. There had already been a reduction of personnel and squadrons based at the airfield. By mid-December most of RAF aircraft and personal had left, although the airfield equipment was kept in place. The airfield was earmarked for care and maintenance, and was not idle for long, as on 1 January 1946 it was transferred to Admiralty control as a Royal Naval Air Station.

Chapter 4

Royal Navy Presence

Brawdy Airfield only remained idle for a brief period as on 1 January 1946 it was officially transferred to Admiralty control as a naval air station. The Royal Navy was short of large airfields with reasonably lengthed runways for their twin-engined training aircraft. Most of the Admiralty airfields at the time were used mainly for the use of carrier-based aircraft while their hosts were in dock or being refitted. Brawdy was commissioned HMS Goldcrest II, a RLG (Relief Landing Ground) or, in naval parlance, a 'tender airfield', for Goldcrest I, the RNAS at Dale, another former RAF station.

The Admiralty acquired RAF Dale on 1 September 1943, when it exchanged the airfield for its base across the Haven at Angle. Between February 1944 and August 1945 Dale became one of the navy's busiest shore bases, involved in twin-engine training and squadron conversions to Supermarine Seafire LIICs, Fairey Firefly Mk7s and the American Corsairs. Admiralty personnel at Brawdy were limited to a skeleton staff for fire and rescue, refuelling, security, flight control and, as from December 1946, No.811 Squadron personnel.

At the time Dale was home to the naval night fighting school, equipped with Grumman Hellcats II, Avro Ansons and DH Mosquitoes of No.748 Squadron RN. Also at Dale was the training and conversion unit, No.790 Squadron, equipped with Fairey Firefly Mk7s. Both squadrons made use of the spacious facilities at Brawdy.

The only squadron based at Brawdy was No.811, the only DH Sea Mosquito TR33 squadron in naval service. Taking up residence on 6 December 1946, they departed for Eglinton on 30 March 1947. The Sea Mosquito TR33 was a variant of the FBVI, fitted with an arrester gear, folding wings and four bladed propellers, and armed with four 20mm cannon and a bomb (mine or torpedo) load of 2,000lb. A converted

Mosquito VI with an arrester gear made the first deck landing on the aircraft carrier HMS *Indefatigable* on 25 March 1944, but the first production model did not fly until November 1945.

Another unit to be based at Brawdy during this eighteen-month period was the Royal Aircraft Establishment Pilotless Aircraft Unit, which worked in co-operation the Dale-based squadrons. This unit operated Miles M50 Queen Martinets, a radio-controlled version of the Martinet TT Mk1.

Also while under Admiralty control an RAF radio meteorological flight consisting of six Airspeed Oxfords was based at the airfield between January and July 1946.

In June 1947 the airfield was closed and put on care and maintenance under Admiralty control. The airfield at Dale was also closed on 13 December 1947.

Pleased with their previous operations from the airfield, and the prospect of expansion, the Admiralty decided to retain the airfield as a shore base for carrier aircraft while their hosts were in dock, as well as for training and conversions.

The airfield remained on care and maintenance for five years, during which work began on the expansion phase.

Re-commissioning as an active naval air station occurred on 4 September 1952, although work was not completed until the following year.

The first squadron to be reformed at Brawdy was No.849, on 7 July 1952, equipped with Douglas Skyraider AEW Is. Aircraft and personnel arrived at a base, which resembled a building site rather than an airfield. Through all the inconvenience operations carried on functioning normally, and the squadron was to remain at Brawdy throughout, until its closure in December 1971.

The first frontline naval unit to arrive at HMS Goldcrest II after re-commissioning was No.804 Squadron on 3 November 1952, equipped with Hawker Sea Fury FBIIs.

Line up of Hawker Sea Fury FB11s of No.802 Squadron at the naval air station.

Aerial view of the airfield showing alterations done by the Admiralty. (Via RNAS Brawdy)

The squadron remained at Brawdy until 16 January 1953, when it was deployed aboard the aircraft carrier HMS *Indomitable*.

The following is a summary, in numerical order, of the naval squadrons and their aircraft based at Brawdy between 1952 and 1971:

No.727 Training Squadron was a resident unit at the naval air station from 4 January 1956 to 16 December 1960, when it was disbanded. It was equipped with Sea Balliols, Sea Princes and Sea Vampires for jet training.

No.736 Squadron was equipped with Fleet Air Arm supersonic fighters, Supermarine Scimitar F1s, and was based for training at Brawdy from 4 June to 2 July 1960, although some of its aircraft re-visited West Wales during the naval air days.

No.738 Squadron visited Brawdy on a regular basis, especially when carriers were in dock. The squadron's first visit was in November 1954, followed by others in 1956, 1957, 1958, and 1959. No.738 Squadron was equipped with various marks of the Armstrong

The Sea Balliol became a standard training aircraft with the Royal Naval Air Service in the early fifties and served with No.727 Squadron. (Via RNAS Brawdy)

De Havilland Vampire of No.727 Squadron.

Line up of naval Sea Hawks in front of Brawdy's tower.

The first naval jet fighter was the Supermarine Attacker, which proved to be no faster than the later marks of Sea Fire or the Sea Fury, and was therefore reallocated to a training roll. The photograph shows Attackers operated by Airwork Ltd in storage at St David's, Brawdy's satellite airfield.

A neat line up of DH Vampires of Airwork Ltd at St David's. (S. Broomfield)

Whitworth Sea Hawk naval fighter-bombers. In the early sixties the squadron was disbanded and reformed as a training unit at Lossiemouth. However, in 1964 No.738, equipped with Hawker Hunter T8 and GA 11s, was transferred to Brawdy were it remained until 1970. The squadron was responsible for training naval pilots on a twelve-week basis, and included tactical formation flying, simulated air-to-air gunnery and air-to-ground raids with both cannon and rockets. Also, it trained pilots in air-to-air combat as well as low-level flying (similar to the role of RAF No.1 TWU).

A detachment from No.751 Squadron was based at Brawdy from 13–15 May 1957, equipped first with North American Avenger AS4s, then, for its next visit from 11–19 September 1957, with DH Sea Venoms.

No.759 Squadron, equipped with Hawker Hunter T8s and T8Cs, arrived at Brawdy on 1 August 1963 and remained until 24 December 1967. This eventually became the last Fleet Air Arm squadron to be permanently based at Brawdy.

No.800 Squadron was another naval unit that visited the base on a regular basis from November 1954, while aircraft carriers were in dock. The types of aircraft operated by the squadron were various marks of Armstrong Whitworth (Hawker) Sea Hawks.

No.801 Squadron were resident at Brawdy between 1957 and 1960, and were equipped with Sea Hawk F1, F2 and FGA6s.

No.802 Squadron was deployed aboard HMS *Theseus*, but while the carrier was in dock, between 12 May and 16 June 1953, resided at Brawdy equipped with Hawker Sea Fury FB 11s.

Above and below: A Hunting Sea Prince of Brawdy's station flight.

Aerial view of Brawdy's technical site in 1954. (Welsh Assembly Government)

No.804 Squadron was another unit equipped with Sea Hawk FGA6s, and was based at the airfield from August to September 1959.

No.806 Squadron was the first naval squadron to be equipped with jet aircraft, Hawker Sea Hawk F1s, and was based at Brawdy from 2 March 1953 to 5 ebruary 1954. Most of the necessary conversions were done at the base before the Sea Hawks entered into a naval carrier.

No.807 Squadron made station history as the first naval jet squadron to be based at Brawdy equipped with Sea Hawks. The squadron arrived at Brawdy on 10 May 1954 to be re-equipped with Sea Hawks. Further visits by the squadron took place between 19 February and 3 March 1955, with its last occurring in July 1955.

X Flight of No.813 Squadron was based at the airfield from 18 March 1957 to 5 April 1957, and again from 20 May to 5 August 1957. The squadron was equipped with the turbo-powered Westland Wyvern S4 strike aircraft, which were deployed on

Brawdy's first station flight helicopter was a Westland Dragonfly.

Prior to the entry into service of the Fairey Gannet, No.849 Squadron at Brawdy operated several Douglas Skyraiders in AEW roles.

No.849 Squadron was a resident at Brawdy from 1959–70, equipped with Fairey Gannet anti-submarine aircraft. Photograph shows the Airborne Early Warning version in flight.

Fairey Gannet AS4 (277) inside one of the air station's hangars.

A Gannet AS4 being prepared for flight. (S. Broomfield)

A line up of Gannet AEWs of No.849 Squadron.

An unusual black–painted Gannet AS4 used for electronic countermeasure training and designated ECM6. (Via RNAS Brawdy)

A mass take off of Hawker Sea Hawks. (Via D. Edwards)

Typical Royal Navy startup of Sea Hawks of No.898 Squadron, October 1956.

Smoke arising from a startup of Sea Hawks belonging to 897 Squadron.

West German Air Force Noratlas transport aircraft were regular visitors to Brawdy during the sixties, in support of West German Army training at Castlemartin. (Via WGAF)

A visiting DH Venom FAW21 at Brawdy.

Hawker Hunter GA11s of No.738 Squadron were used for ground attack and air-to-air combat roles.

The Tiger Moth T2 remained part of the station flight until the naval air station closed. (S. Broomfield)

Another view of a Hawker Hunter GA11 of No.738 Squadron.

A Hawker Hunter T8 of No.759 Squadron, a sister unit to No.738, in a tactical training role.

Brawdy's station flight also consisted of three Westland Whirlwind HAS7s for SAR duties.

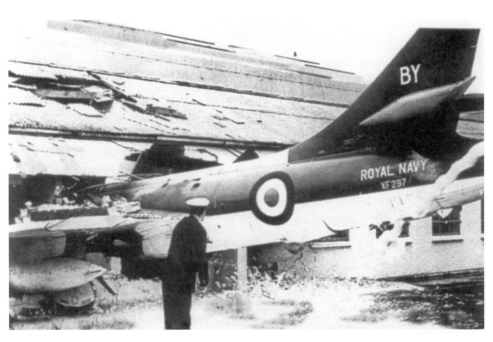

Hunter GA11 XF297 crashed into one of Brawdy's hangars following a landing mishap. (Via HMS Goldcrest)

The Turbine-powered Westland Whirlwind HAR9 replaced the piston-engined HAS7 on SAR duties.

H. M. S. Goldcrest

Royal Naval Air Station Brawdy

Ceremony to mark the Transfer of

Royal Naval Air Station Brawdy

to the Royal Air Force

The official invitation to the hand over ceremony from the Fleet Air Arm to the RAF on 1 April 1974.

on Thursday, 1st April, 1971

the aircraft carrier HMS *Eagle*. Between four and six were stationed at Brawdy, and were regularly seen practising attacks on the Preseli hills around the coast.

No.824 Squadron, equipped with Fairey Gannet AS1s, was based at the airfield between 7 June and 1 July 1955. The Fairey Gannet replaced the Avenger, Firefly and Douglas Skyraiders on anti-submarine duties for the Fleet Air Arm.

No.831 A and B Flights were resident from 16–19 November 1964, with Sea Venoms and Sea Princes for training and familiarisation operations.

No.849 Squadron was more or less permanently based at Brawdy, especially from 1959 to 1970. The squadron moved from RNAS Culdrose on 15 December 1964, but initially the squadron was formed at Brawdy in 1959 and equipped with Douglas Skyraiders. The squadron was on carrier airborne early warning duties – exactly what the task force lacked during the Falklands War – and provided anti-submarine capability.

Brawdy at this time served two functions: supplying an operational element to the fleet and fulfilling the squadron's training role. The squadron was equipped with various marks of the turbo-powered Fairey Gannet, which replaced the Skyraider and the Firefly.

No.849 Squadron was split up, with it HQ at Brawdy, and A, B, C, and D Flights on the carriers:

A Flight was deployed on HMS *Victorious*.
B Flight was deployed on HMS *Centaur*.
C Flight was deployed on HMS *Ark Royal*.
D Flight was deployed on HMS *Eagle*.

Each carrier flight consisted of four AEW3s, four AS1s and one COD4, while Brawdy (HQ) flight consisted of three AEWs, three ASs, two CODs and five T5s, not including reserve aircraft.

There were four versions of the Gannet in service with No.849 Squadron. The AEW3 version was fitted with an AN/APS radar dome under the fuselage, the AS4 version was used on anti-submarine duties, and the COD4 for fleet transport. This latter variant was used on carrier-to-carrier and carrier-to-shore duties, and could carry two passengers in the aft seats along with mail and essential equipment in special racks in the bomb bay. The T5 was a training model used for anti-submarine operations, operating radar, conversion training and weapon use. Torpedo and depth charge exercises were carried out in Cardigan Bay under the control of RAE Aberporth.

When the carrier force was reduced in 1970, by September only two flights remained: B and D, which operated airborne early warning duties aboard HMS *Ark Royal* and HMS *Eagle*, as well as the HQ Flight at Brawdy.

A few of the surplus Gannet AS4s based at Brawdy were converted for electronic countermeasure training, and painted black.

No.849 Squadron left HMS Goldcrest II on 19 November 1970, headed for RNAS Lossiemouth in Scotland.

No.891 Squadron resided at Brawdy from 2 March to 14 March 1956, with DH Sea Venom FAW 21s.

No.892 Squadron was equipped with DH Sea Vixen FAW2s, and was only based at Brawdy for one naval exercise lasting from 21 August to 9 September 1956.

No.893 Squadron was another DH Sea Venom FAW21 unit, and was stationed at Brawdy between 6 and 24 October 1959.

No.895 Squadron was formed at Brawdy on 23 April 1956, equipped with Sea Hawk FGA4s and 6s. The squadron personnel, despite having arrived some months before, did not receive the aircraft until April. After intensive training the squadron was declared operational on 25 June 1956.

In early August the squadron was deployed on HMS *Bulwark*. The ground crew travelled by train from Haverfordwest to Portsmouth to join the carrier, while the twelve aircraft flew out days afterwards to join the ship in the Channel, destined for the Mediterranean in preparation for the invasion of Suez.

No.898 Squadron was the second naval squadron to be re-equipped with pure jet aircraft, Hawker Sea Hawks, and was stationed at Brawdy during August 1963.

The squadron was re-formed at the Royal Naval Air Station on 24 August 1953, and left later in the year to embark on the aircraft carrier HMS *Albion*.

No.831 Squadron was a training and conversion unit stationed at Brawdy between 28 July and 10 August 1956, equipped with Sea Balliol trainers, Sea Vampires and Supermarine Attackers.

During the naval presence at Brawdy there was the resident station helicopter rescue service. In the early days the search and rescue Flight was equipped with the Westland Dragonfly, then with the Westland Whirlwind HAS2 and eventually the turbine-powered Whirlwind HAR9.

In 1958 the future of Brawdy was in doubt once again as the Government announced the decommission of the navy aircraft carriers, and therefore a general run down of naval fixed wing aircraft. However, after a two-year revision, the plan was modified and the airfield was reprieved. The station status as a support base for frontline forces had diminished and its future role was to be involved in advance training.

Between 1961 and 1963 there was, once again, an extensive modernisation programme initiated to accommodate the new breed of jet aircraft that were entering service with the Fleet Air Arm, such as the Sea Vixen and the Scimitar, and eventually the Blackburn Buccaneer (see Chapter Two).

After the latest round of modernisation, flying activity resumed on 1 August 1963 when No.759 was commissioned at the airfield. The squadron was equipped with nine two-seat Hawker Hunter T8s and a single-seat GA11. The unit was joined on 1 January 1964 by No.738 Squadron from RNAS Lossiemouth, with its fleet of Hunters mainly made up of GA11s and four T8s.

Both squadrons were involved in advance flying training with conversion from the Jet Provost to more modern jets like the Buccaneer, Sea Vixen and eventually the Phantom.

Before being posted to Brawdy students would complete their basic training at the RAF flying training school flying Chipmunks and, eventually, Jet Provosts, the standard British jet trainer of the time. The next fourteen weeks would be spent with No.759 Squadron completing part one of the advance flying training course.

It also became the base of Royal Navy aircraft support unit. The first part of the course involved logging at least sixty hours in a Hunter, covering all aspects of flying including forced landings and emergencies, formation flying, high speed navigation, low-level flying and even aerobatics. Sadly there were several mishaps and accidents during training, but thankfully fatalities were few.

No.738 Squadron was responsible for the second phase of the training programme, which lasted twelve weeks. It included all aspects of air combat, including ground attack with rockets and bombs, simulated air-to-air combat, low-level strike missions over land and sea, instrument flying. Most of the training was completed in the single-seat GA11s, while the instructor flew in the T8.

The ground attack was usually conducted at the Castlemartin range or on towed barges in Cardigan Bay, while the air gunnery took place over the Cardigan Bay range using target-towing Brawdy-based Meteors provided by RAE Llanbedr.

Once the student completed the course he would be posted to a naval conversion unit equipped with Buccaneers or Sea Vixens.

In 1967 HMS Goldcrest II provided a land base for the Fleet Air Arm Buccaneer strike-bombers of Nos 736 and 800 Squadrons during the Torrey Canyon disaster. On 18 March 1967 the 118,000-ton oil tanker, the *Torrey Canyon*, ran aground the Seven Stones Reef, off the Cornish coast, in bad weather. Large amounts of crude oil were washed ashore, but the majority remained on board the stricken vessel. An unwise decision at the time, it was thought best to sink the ship with bombs and burn the oil with napalm. Twelve naval Buccaneer S2s armed with 1,000lb bombs operated out of Brawdy. After the initial attack by the Buccaneers the ship sank, and was soon followed by napalm strikes by RAF Hunters from Chivenor, to burn off the oil that had collected on the surface. It might not have been the best way of dealing with spilt crude oil, but it gave the aircrew a rare opportunity to attack and sink a surface vessel.

By the late sixties the Royal Navy's carrier force was down to three fleet carriers, HMS *Hermes*, *Eagle* and *Ark Royal*. With the scrapping of the last aircraft carrier, the *Ark Royal*, naval presence at Brawdy was coming to an end. The last course was completed in November 1969 with the students leaving to join the remaining FAA frontline squadrons.

No.759 Squadron was the first to be decommissioned on 24 December 1969, followed by No.738. By 8 May 1970 all the Hunter squadrons and their personnel had left the base. The only unit to remain was No.849 with its Gannet aircraft, until it too departed for Lossiemouth on 19 December 1970. Ironically, the last ever naval training flight from Brawdy was performed in No.849 Squadron's Gannet aircraft on 1 December.

Brawdy also had its own station flight consisting of two Sea Princes (WP312 and WJ349) in 1967/68, and one Sea Devon for communication duties, three Vampire T22s and three Gloster Meteor T8s, used for target towing and re-training, and a Tiger Moth (BB694) for cadet 'familiarity' flights. Some of the station flight aircraft had been at Brawdy since the late fifties, when the Vampires and Meteors were often used in exercises with the Territorial Army who had their summer camps in the Preseli area on the Castle Martin tank range. The author remembers the screams of the jets during their mock attacks on camouflaged Territorial Army vehicles. In a nearby village one old lady shut herself in a cupboard under the stairs, perhaps recalling the wartime advice to hide under the stairs during an air raid.

A single Supermarine Scimitar F1 (XD219) was also based with the maintenance test pilot's school, and underwent various modifications and assessments with new equipment.

Admiralty control of the airfield came to an end in January 1971. By this date all naval property had been removed and distributed to various destinations.

Since 1949 Airwork Ltd had a depot in Pembrokeshire and was contracted out by the Admiralty to undertake conversion-training courses on heavy twin-engine aircraft. Although using naval aircraft, the unit was entirely staffed by civilian pilots and ground crews, sourced locally. Airwork Ltd was also responsible for providing radar targets for interception training missions under the control of the aircraft direction centre at HMS Harrier, Kete. Originally the unit was equipped with DH Sea Mosquitoes and Sea Hornets, but later was re-equipped with Sea Venoms, Meteor T7s and Attackers. The unit moved to St David's Airfield, by now Brawdy's satellite, in September 1951. However, they returned to Brawdy in October 1958 when space became available, before eventually moving to Yeovilton when the base closed.

It is worth noting that another unit based at Brawdy was the Naval Aircraft Support Unit (NASU), occupying the three new interconnecting hangars. This unit, with its 300-plus personnel, moved from RNAS Abbotsinch in 1963. NASU was responsible for providing aircraft for frontline operations, over-haul and repair work, fitting modifications to aircraft and then flight-testing them, which was the work of the maintenance test pilot's school. Aircraft storage was another responsibility of the unit as several naval aircraft were mothballed and stored in a humidity-free environment. Aircraft awaiting disposal were usually stored at Brawdy's satellite station at St David's.

A typical example of the NASU workload between 1967 and 1968 includes issuing a total of 130 aircraft to various units within the Fleet Air Arm. The type of aircraft varied, but included Scimitars, Sea Vixen, various marks of the Fairey Gannet, both Hunter T7 and 8s, Sea Devons and Sea Herons.

By 1969 NASU importance had diminished and the unit was gradually reduced, many of its personnel being posted to other stations – although some aircraft were kept in storage until the base closed.

Following the Government decision to decommission the navy aircraft carriers, the last being HMS *Ark Royal*, scheduled for late 1970s, the FAA presence at Brawdy was coming to an end. Throughout 1970 the Admiralty removed most of its equipment, leaving a small naval contingent of both servicemen and women and civilians, up until 1 April 1971 when the base tenure was returned to the Ministry of Defence.

From 1971 to '74 the Department of Environment maintained the base, and no flying took place.

With the threat of a Soviet attack on the west in the 1950s and '60s, it was arranged for the British V bomber force to be dispersed to thirty-six airfields throughout the UK. This was to give the island protection from a surprise attack; a maintained Quick Reaction Alert (QRA) team could be airborne within two and a half minutes. In

Wales three airfields were classed as QRA bases: RAF Valley on Anglesey, the RAE airfield at Llanbedr and RNAS Brawdy in Pembrokeshire.

During redevelopment at Brawdy between 1961 and 1963, new hard standing pads were built on the end of the lengthened runway 21 to accommodate the V bombers and the various ground equipment that was now permanently stored at the naval air station. In event of a rise in threat two or three V-bombers (most probably Vulcans) together with ground crew would fly in to await orders.

For a brief period towards the end of the 1960s Brawdy was host to a contingent of the Luftwaffe (the West German Air Force) who were based at the airfield while the German Army and their Leopard battle tanks were on exercises at Castlemartin tank range. The tanks were unloaded from landing crafts on Freshwater West beach while the troops were flown in to Brawdy in Nord Noratlas transport aircraft. In 1967 a squadron of West German Fiat G91 fighter-bombers made a lengthy visit to the base for weapon evaluation and ground attack training with the tanks at Castlemartin. At the time there was considerable hostilities towards the Germans in Pembrokeshire, but under NATO obligations they were allowed to train in the UK. However, after the initial hostility the Welsh people accepted them.

The German detachment at Brawdy consisted of air force maintenance and movement personnel to deal with the regular Noratlas service bringing mail, spare parts and army personnel from Germany.

During the summer of 1959 the aircraft carrier HMS *Bulwark*, which had just recently completed a refit and conversion to a commando carrier, conducted trials off the coast of Pembrokeshire. After the Suez Crisis of 1956 it was realised that the Royal Navy had a requirement for ships that could embark Royal Marine units, with all their equipment, to be dispatched to trouble spots, and be capable of disembarking either by landing craft or helicopter. As HMS *Bulwark* was surplus to requirement and was not earmarked for a major refit it was converted to the new role. The carrier, first launched in 1948, was converted for its commando role at Portsmouth Dockyard in early 1959. It could carry up to 600 RM commandos and up to sixteen Westland Whirlwind helicopters or twelve of the later Wessex helicopters. Also, the carrier had four assault landing crafts on davits.

While HMS *Bulwark* was anchored in St Brides Bay, Whirlwind helicopters transported commandoes and their equipment ashore to the airfield, including lightweight Humber trucks and Land Rovers slung beneath. Two of Brawdy's Whirlwinds took part in the exercise.

During its period in Pembrokeshire the navy could boast of a remarkable safety record compared with other bases in the UK. Admittedly there were a few fatalities, but most were minor mishaps. One such accident happened during a mass take off of Sea Hawks from No.898 Squadron, when a drop take came off one aircraft and hit another causing it to swerve and skid onto the grass where it came to rest without any injury to its crew. Another involved a Mosquito belonging to the Airwork service that was unable to stop when taxiing and crashed into a parked Sea Hornet causing considerable damage to both. Another occurred on Thursday 20 November 1969 when a Hawker Hunter XF297/BY of the 'Diamonds' aerobatic team crashed into a hangar.

Petty Officer George Hankin and his team was conducting an engine test as during an earlier flight the pilot had reported problems with the aircraft's Rolls Royce Avon turbo jet. Common procedure was to ground run the engine while the diagnosis took place. The Hunter, with Petty Officer Hankin in the pilot seat, jumped the chocks and careered some seventy-five yards across the apron before embedding itself in the side of a hangar. Luckily the engine flamed out and Petty Officer Hankin was pulled out of the aircraft unhurt, if rather shocked.

Another incident recalled by one rating involved the station's commanding officer. Taxiing his Meteor T8 after a flight, he clipped his wing against the station's Sea Prince fuselage while it was being towed into a hangar. Both aircraft received only minimal damage and were airworthy again within days. The embarrassing incident was never recorded in the station's log!

Brawdy also played the part of a civilian airport when, in 1958, the London-based Morton Air Service expressed an interest in establishing an air service between Pembrokeshire and London (Croydon Airport). Withybush, Haverfordwest, was the first choice, but the aerodrome was found to be derelict and unusable. Therefore, the operation was moved to the military airfield at Brawdy. The Admiralty provided a building to be used as a passenger waiting room that included refreshments as required. The daily service was introduced to the public in April 1958, with a stop at Fairwood Common for Swansea.

The first service via Swansea was inaugurated on 2 June 1959 by DH Heron G-AOGO. Subsequent stops at Swansea were only made when traffic demanded. Gatwick replaced Croydon as the premier London destination in October 1959, and the last Croydon flight from Swansea was on 29 September 1959 by DH Dove G-ANAN. The load factor was not impressive even after the airline provided a bus link service with Haverfordwest, used mainly by naval officers.

There was always an extraordinary bond between all the personnel that served in the Fleet Air Arm at Brawdy, so much so that several websites have been formed to keep members informed as to their whereabouts. At the time of writing the Royal Navy Association's HMS Goldcrest section membership exceeds 2,000 ex-naval personnel – men and women who were based at Brawdy and have kept that comradeship alive.

Chapter 5

The RAF Period
1971–1995

From 1971 to 1974 the base came under the control of the Department of Environment with its future in doubt. However, a Government defence review decided that the RAF would use the airfield after all, although at the time its role had not been verified. Eventually it was decided to use the base for operational conversion training.

The RAF took control of the airfield in January 1974 after a modest modernisation programme.

The official ceremony to mark the transfer of the airfield was held on Thursday 1 April 1974, with the Lord Lieutenant of Pembrokeshire accompanied by Group Captain Radley RAF and Commander Cowan RN, who all inspected the parade. There were marched past with the Royal Marines band providing the music. After a fly past by Fleet Air Arm aircraft from RNAS Yeovilton, prayers were said followed by a ceremonial sunset, reveille and the two National Anthems, Hen Wlad Fy Nhadau and God Save the Queen. On completion Commander Cowan RN ceremonially confided the air station to the Royal Air Force, then all the dignitaries and guests proceeded to reception room for refreshments.

The RAF first commanding officer was Acting Squadron Leader A.B. Clark who commanded the base during the transition phase.

The first RAF unit to use the base was D Flight of No.22 Squadron, with its search and rescue Westland Whirlwind HAR 10 helicopters.

It was not until 4 September 1974 that No.229 OCU, equipped with Hawker Hunter T8s, moved in to their new base from RAF Chivenor. This unit was eventually

Aerial photograph of Brawdy Airfield, 1983. (Welsh Assembly Government)

Hawker Hunter FGA9 (XG194) of No.79 Squadron.

Hawker Hunter FGA9 of No.79 Squadron landing using a parachute brake. (No.79 Squadron Archives)

1 Miles Martinet TT1 of No.595 Squadron.

2 BAe Hawk trainers replaced the Hunters of the tactical weapons unit. The photograph shows a BAe Hawk T1.

3 A BAe Hawk T1 of 1 TWU flying over the beautiful Pembrokeshire coast. (Via RAF Brawdy)

4 One of Brawdy's B Flight of No.202 Squadron Sea King SAR helicopters flying over the Pembrokeshire countryside. (Via RAF Brawdy)

5 A BAe Hawk of No.234 squadron 1 TWU painted to commemorate the unit's seventy-fifth anniversary over the Pembrey range. (Via RAF Brawdy)

6 No.1 TWU Hawk on a dusk sortie over the sea. (Via RAF Brawdy)

7 Brawdy's SAR helicopters were constantly training with RNLI lifeboats.

8 Humour has always played a part in the navy air displays; whether that is a witch flying a broomstick slung under a helicopter or a person riding a mockup of a Russian missile. (D. Edwards)

9 A German Air Force Lockheed Starfighter was a frequent visitor to Brawdy' air displays.

10 Red Arrows famous bomb blast.

11 Panavia Tornado GR1 of No.27 Squadron making a low-level high-speed pass over the airfield.

A line up of various marks of Hunters belonging to TWU. (Via RAF Brawdy)

A Hawker Hunter FGA9 of No.79 Squadron over the Pembrokeshire coast. (No.79 Squadron Archives)

Group Captain Douglas Bader visits TWU in August 1978. (Via Dr Middleton)

RAF McDonnell Douglas Phantom F4 at Brawdy, 1986.

RAF Hercules transport aircraft were regular visitors to the airfield.

A Hawk, two Meteors, a Jet Provost and a Hunter of 1 TWU in flight. (Via RAF Brawdy)

A Buccaneer S2 of No.237 OCU landing at Brawdy.

BAe Hawk T1 (XX192) of 1 TWU, photographed in March 1978. This aircraft crashed near the airfield in September 1989.

re-named No.1 Tactical Weapons Unit (1 TWU) with its sister unit No.2 TWU based at Lossiemouth.

Tactical Weapons Unit was responsible for training RAF operational pilots in the skills of air combat, air-to-ground attack and tactical low flying, which was a regular occurrence over the Pembrokeshire's countryside. In a small way Brawdy's history was repeating itself as twenty years earlier the Fleet Air Arm Nos 738 and 759 Squadrons were doing the same sort of training.

No.229 OCU consisted of three shadow squadrons, Nos 63, 79 and later 234, all equipped with 100 various marks of Hawker Hunters and eight Gloster Meteors.

No.79 Squadron operated Hunter FGA9s, FR10s and T7s, with Gloster Meteor T7s and T8s used for target towing duties, while Nos 63 and 234 Squadrons were equipped with Hunter F6 and T7s.

By 1974 the Hawker Hunter had been in service with the RAF for twenty years. It was a firm favourite with the pilots and ground crew.

The Hawker Hunter first flew in July 1954 and over 1,000 aircraft were built for the RAF alone. The Hunter was powered by a single Rolls Royce Avon 200/3 jet engine of 10,000lb thrust, which gave it a top speed of 715mph and a range of 1,846 miles. The fighter and ground attack version was armed with four Aden 30mm cannons and a 2,000lb bomb load.

No.63 and 234 Squadrons utilised their Hunters F6 and T7s for air-to-air gunnery both at high and low level, using either other Hunters or Meteors to simulate combat conditions. Live firing was done using towed targets over the Cardigan Bay test range. No.79 Squadron's Hunter FGA9 and FR10s were used for air-to-ground weapon firing, ground attack training with bombs, rocket and cannon and tactical low-level flying, as well as operating refresher courses for pilots. All the live weapons tests usually took place at the Pembrey range.

Pilots would graduated from the Flying School at Valley to TWU, and after completing the course they would be posted to an Operational Conversion Unit flying Buccaneers, Harriers, Phantoms and Tornadoes.

In June 1978 the tactical weapons unit was split into two sections: No.1 at Brawdy, and No.2 TWU at RAF Lossiemouth in Scotland, equipped with surplus Hunters from Brawdy. However, due to Lossiemouth being chosen as a Nimrod/Shakleton and Buccaneer base used for anti-shipping duties, the airfield became congested and space was at a premium. In 1980 the unit returned to Brawdy and to the re-opened airfield at Chivenor, which eventually became the home of No.2 TWU. The British Aerospace Hawk was initially meant as a replacement for the Jet Provost and Folland Gnat that had been the RAF main training aircraft hereto, but the aircraft's towering potential meant it could fill the gap between jet training and conversion units.

The BAe Hawk T1/1A is powered by a Rolls Royce Turbomeca Adour turbo fan of 5,200lb, giving the aircraft a speed of 633mph.

In 1978 the Hawk T1 replaced the TWU Hunter, but the phase in was gradual and for a time both types operated side by side. The first Hawks to be handed over to Brawdy were XX187 and XX190 on 4 December 1977 in a ceremony attended by the RAF, Ministry of Defence and representatives from BAe. The local press also covered the event. Over the next few months the two aircraft were thoroughly checked out by the training instructors. Certain modifications were noted and passed to the manufacturer, which were then included in the next batch delivered. Throughout 1978 Hawks were delivered to Brawdy, and the Hunters were eventually phased out. Some of the aircraft remained with TWU replacing the Meteors, but most were returned to British Aerospace or to storage at St Athan.

Tactical weapons unit had a total of thirty-six Hawks on charge, plus surplus spares, and were housed in the airfield's T2 hangars. Initially the aircraft were painted in the usual green and grey over-all camouflage pattern, but this was changed to an air superiority grey finish. The Hawk proved a superb training aircraft and became a firm favourite with its instructors and students, just like its predecessor. No. 1 TWU also had a number of Hunter T7 and Jet Provost T4s on strength, which were used for refresher training for service personnel. The Hawk trainer replaced both types.

About seventy-two Hawks from Nos 1 and 2 TWU were armed with two Aden 30mm cannons in under-wing pods and two Sidewinder air-to-air missiles that could be used as secondary defence in a war situation. The Mk T1As would be deployed to other UK airfields for secondary air defence. Six would remain at Brawdy.

In October 1979 No.22 Search and Rescue Squadron was replaced by Westland Sea Kings HAR3 of B Flight (No.202 Squadron). This search and rescue squadron was reformed in September 1964 with Whirlwind helicopters. Detached flights were based at Acklington, Coltishall and Leuchars, with HQ at RAF Leconfield, Yorkshire. Following a reorganisation the headquarters was moved to RAF Finningley on 1 January 1976. In 1979 No.202 Squadron was re-equipped with the Westland Sea King, an all-weather machine that gave the unit double the range and endurance of the Whirlwinds. B Flight, with two helicopters, was formed in October 1979 at Brawdy to provide search and rescue services to West Wales and beyond.

The Westland Sea King HAR3 is derived from a United States Navy anti-submarine helicopter designed and built by Sikorsky Aircraft Corporation. The helicopter was built under licence by Westland Aircraft for the Royal Navy. Seeing its potential the RAF ordered a SAR version in late 1970, to replace the Whirlwind.

The anglicised version is powered by two Rolls Royce Gnome gas turbine engines of 2,778-shaft horsepower driving a five-bladed main rotor. Its radius of action is well over 250 miles with a maximum speed of 144mph.

The squadron badge signifies its close relation with the sea, for it shows a mallard duck alighting, with the motto 'Semper Vigilate', meaning 'be always vigilant'.

The flight covered most of Wales, south-west England and the western approaches of the Atlantic. Tasks included rescuing crew from sinking ships and swimmers in difficulty, assisting mountain rescue teams, performing overland searches for missing people and doing relief work.

During the Falklands conflict in 1982 a Sea King helicopter of No.202 Squadron, from RAF Brawdy, was detached to Wideawake Airfield on Ascension Island to provide search and rescue cover during the intensive air activity that took place there. When the Sea King was not employed on its primary duty, it was involved in the seemingly never-ending work of transferring stores between the base and supply ships, and between supply ships and warships.

Every year pilots and instructors of No.1 TWU compete for the Prince of Wales Trophy, which is designed to test the operational skills of tactical low-level flying and of various weapons. The competition was first held in 1980 and quickly became a popular event among the aircrews. As 1992 was the last year of the competition, HRH Prince Charles, Prince of Wales, made an appreciated gesture by attending the award ceremony, held on 29 May 1992.

The joint winners of the trophy were Flight Lieutenants 'Crusty' Cobb and Al Monkman, both of No.79 Squadron, who got the same score – which was very unusual.

The competition was opened to all RAF squadrons flying fast jets, but the trophy is only available to pilots of the BAe Hawk trainers. In 1992 there were thirty-four aircraft taking part in the competition including Hawks from No.1 TWU sister unit at Chivenor.

It was a tough competition and the contenders had to complete six tasks including flying a reconnaissance mission over an enemy airbase, attacking a column of armoured vehicles and obtaining a film of the attack, reconnaissance flight in search of enemy vehicles (usually in mid-Wales) and low-level flying at precisely 250ft above the ground. Then they had to obtain a reconnaissance film of a radar site, following a simulated enemy attack by aircraft, culminating in weapon training with practise bomb and strafe attacks with Aden cannons on the Pembrey weapons range. All tasks had to be verified by gun camera film.

The tasks in the competition were exactly the tasks undertaken by TWU in normal training and were tasks required operationally.

Brawdy was also used as a forward operating base for RAF Phantom aircraft. Several hard standing pads with their own starting units were allocated to the Phantoms and on many occasions detachments of Phantoms were regularly seen at the airfield.

Another resident at the base was the United States Navy Oceanographic Research Unit operated by USNAVFAC. This secretive unit was situated away from the airfield's operational side, just off the entrance road to the base. Even after the base shut its existence was often denied.

In January 1992 the Ministry of Defence announced another defence review, and after a careful assessment decided to cease all flying training at Brawdy. This was a drastic blow to the county and to the personnel station at the airfield as so many had made roots in the area.

The last training flight took place on 28 August 1992 by ten Hawks. It marked a sad day in the history of both squadrons as that year No.79 and 234 Squadrons celebrated their seventy-fifth anniversaries.

The Hawk safety record was and still is impressive, bearing in mind training units tended to have a higher accident rate than other squadrons. Only three Hawk T1s were written off in accidents during the time they were based at Brawdy. Accidents involving Hunters were three times that number, but it must be remembered that the Hunters had accumulated high flying hours prior to being transferred to Brawdy.

One accident occurred on 4 May 1976 when Hunter F6 (XJ 635) of No.1 TWU crashed at Moriah in mid-Wales. Flying Officer Irvin accompanied by an instructor in another Hunter were both on a low-level cross-country flight. Both aircraft followed the coastline just north of Aberystwyth before turning inland. Within few minutes, at 500ft, they encountered low cloud. Both pilots were ordered to return to base, and the two Hunters turned towards the coast. However, Flying Officer Irvin became disorientated as he emerged from the cloud at nearly 450 knots, and was unable to distinguish the horizon.

While at a very low-level, and at an angle, he initiated the ejection procedure, but the drogue had only partially been deployed.

The pilot was instantly killed and the aircraft exploded on impact.

The first Hawk accident was on 29 July 1983 when XX229 crashed into the Irish Sea some fifty miles from the airfield. The student pilot was on a low-level exercise over the sea when he had an engine failure. He ejected safely, sustaining the usual facial cuts and slight back injury, common for pilots ejecting. The Ministry of Defence chartered a Milford Haven trawler to locate the crashed Hawk. It was eventually found in 400ft of water and, after a prolonged salvage operation, certain parts of the aircraft were recovered. However, parts of the engine found indicated that the turbine blades were damaged, which would have resulted in an engine failure.

The second Hawk, XX197, crashed on take off at Brawdy on 13 May 1988. When the aircraft was about 150ft the crew of two, Flt Lt Passfield and Squadron Leader Alan Threadgold, ejected safely, proving yet again the superb record of the Martin Baker Zero Zero ejector seat. The Hawk suffered an engine failure on take off but it seemed the initial momentum made it glide for some distance before crashing into a field outside the airfield's perimeter. According to newspaper reports the aircraft crashed near some unoccupied holiday cottages, spewing out 1,300 kilos of kerosene, which erupted in a fireball.

The last Hawk accident took place on 20 September 1989 and was the most tragic as two of the crew, Flying Officers Alan William George Taylor of Cheltenham and John Patrick Duggan of London, lost their lives. Hawk XX192 was en route to RAF Scampton when the pilot reported a fault. He was advised to return to Brawdy, but on approach to runway 03 crashed into a field.

The cause of the accident was reported as an engine failure. Since then a number of modifications have been made to the Adour engines, which have benefited the flying training schools using the Hawk.

Most of the other incidents involving the aircraft were minor and promptly repaired.

When No.1 TWU was closed both Nos 79 and 234 Squadrons were disbanded and the Hawks distributed between the other squadrons or put in storage.

By the time No.1 TWU was disbanded in 1992, 1,825 students had been trained either on Hunters or Hawks. Several of the students and instructors served in the Falklands campaign and in both the Gulf Wars.

TWU training was highly respected by NATO and other world air forces. In all, nineteen different countries sent students to be trained, mostly as instructors, at Brawdy. As well as the obvious NATO countries, students from the Gulf States, South Africa, New Zealand, Australia and several South American countries were trained by No.1

TWU. Several countries have based their own training programmes on TWU expertise. At the time of writing fast advance flying training and tactical weapon training is done by No.208 and 19 (F) at RAF Valley, and No.100 at RAF Leeming, using Hawk T1/T1As – exactly the same training conducted by No.1 TWU at Brawdy.

Over the rest of the year RAF personnel were gradually reduced: instructors, pilots, ground crew, admin staff, sick quarterlies, mess hall cooks and stewards, radar operators, drivers, suppliers, engineers and mechanics, fitters and general duties staff were posted to other camps and locations.

Fixed wing flying ceased once again. Only B Flight of No.202 Squadron remained at the base as it was essential to keep a search and rescue unit on the west coast of Wales for both military and civilian emergencies. A RAF support unit, together with B Flight personnel, maintained the unit. A reduced emergency service cover was provided and reduced staff ran the control tower. As before the maintenance of the station was the responsibility of a civilian contractor.

In another cost review it was decided that maintaining a SAR unit at Brawdy was uneconomical, and the Ministry of Defence had no future plans for the airfield. So B Flight left Brawdy in late 1996 and all future SAR duties were covered by RAF Chivenor, RNAS Culdrose and RAF Valley. These arrangements were questioned at the time.

Throughout the year all military equipment was removed from the airfield, with a small civilian team maintaining the buildings. Initially it was hoped to keep the runways, hangars and taxiways in good condition, just in case any future review would give the place a reprieve. However, it was decided not to maintain the runways but to concentrate on the buildings.

Brawdy is perhaps one of the best airfields in the UK, and over the years various types of aircraft have used its runways, both military and civilian. During the 1987 general election campaign BAe 748 and BAe One Eleven of the various political parties used the airfield during their visit to the county.

The heaviest aircraft to land anywhere in Pembrokeshire was an USAF Lockheed Galaxy transport aircraft, which was used to fly the United States Navy oceanographic research equipment from their facility at the airfield.

The airfield has close ties with the county: it has provided employment and revenue to local businesses, and over the years thousands of servicemen and women have served at the base and settled in the county, adding to the richness of the community. The base became part of the county, so much so that in 1984 a new station badge was awarded depicting a red sea dragon supporting with one claw the feathers of the Prince of Wales. In the other claw is the sword of strike command. The station lived up to its motto 'Amddiffynfa Y Gorllwein' ('Stronghold in the West').

The last RAF commanding officer, Group Captain Dennis Wilson, remarked that he 'enjoyed the experience and the opportunity to live in one of the loveliest and most welcoming counties in the UK'.

At the time of writing the airfield has been taken over by the army as a base, keeping a military presence in the county. The hangars are used by the army for storage of vehicles and equipment, but as the runways are no longer maintained they have began to break up.

Chapter 6

British Army Present – 14 Signal Regiment

In January 1996 Brawdy became the base for the 14 Signal Regiment, Royal Corp of Signals, and the airfield changed its name to Cawdor Barracks. Preparations had been in place since the RAF left in September 1995, with the unit moving in during December. Cawdor is a name with important local significance as it commemorates the commander of the Pembrokeshire militia which repelled an attempted invasion by the French in 1797.

Like Brawdy itself, 14 Signal Regiment (Electronic Warfare) is unique, as it is the only unit of its type in the British Army. The only other unit conducting similar intelligence and electronic warfare duties is Y Troop, Royal Marines. 14 Signal Regiment of the Royal Corp of Signals provides a wide range of electronic warfare deployments to British and Allied forces in every theatre of operations, from parachute-trained soldiers with man-pack electronic sensors to wheeled and tracked vehicles containing EW equipment. The regiment has nearly 400 vehicles of various descriptions, but the most commonly used is the long wheel-based Land Rover and a modified Warrior tracked vehicle.

14 Signal Regiment (Electronic Warfare) provides a robust electronic warfare capability in support of deployed land commanders, enabling electronic operations in a battle environment. According to military sources the unit is able to jam enemy electronic systems such as communications, radar and target accusation equipment.

The unit is equipped with a vast range of special equipment which can support military operations anywhere in the world. Its soldiers are trained to a very high standard as fighting soldiers and electronic operatives. All soldiers are trained in parachute dropping and are capable of participating in any foot patrol operations.

One of the wheeled vehicles operated by 14 Signal Regiment. (Via MoD)

No.245 Squadron (14 Signal Regiment) also operates tracked vehicles based on Warriors AFV. (Via MoD)

Army Lynx helicopter at Cawdor Barracks, Brawdy.

The army uses the hangars for vehicle and equipment storage, maintenance and indoor training.

14 Signal Regiment (Electronic Warfare) is split into four squadrons: No.226 Signal Squadron (EW), 237 Signal Squadron (EW), 245 Signal Squadron (EW) and Headquarters Squadron.

No.226 Squadron provides EW support to the Allied Command Europe Rapid Reaction Corps, which is also made up of elements from other countries. The squadron operates a wide range of equipment including specialist EW equipment and various computer systems.

No.237 Squadron is assigned to 3 (UK) Division providing a wide range of EW support to the various units. Usually in peacetime the unit provides manpower and equipment for worldwide operations at a short notice. The squadron standard vehicle is the long and short based Land Rover. Also, the squadron provides EW support to 16 Air Assault Brigade.

No.245 Squadron (EW) is assigned to the 1st (UK) Armoured Division, providing the necessary EW support to the armoured regiments of the British army. The squadron is equipped with Armoured Fighting Vehicles (AFV), including variants of the Warrior and Scimitar AFV, as well as soft-skinned support vehicles. The squadron provides men and equipment in support of worldwide operations, which in recent years have been frequent. The unit also has several specialist RAF personnel attached to the squadron.

Finally there is the Headquarter Squadron which is permanently based at Cawdor Barracks and provides all support to the three EW squadrons with administration and logistic. This includes MT (Mechanical Transport), training, stores, technical engineering, medical, welfare and catering. Most of the tasks are provided by other elements in the British Army attached to the Signal Corps. The HQ Squadron is the largest unit of 14 Signal Regiment and is responsible for EW squadrons being deployed around the world with the correct equipment.

Since the end of the second Gulf War No.14 Signals have been actively involved in Iraq and Afghanistan and, sadly, have lost members of the regiment in all the conflicts. Finally, in September 2007, the regiment returned to Cawdor Barracks after a lengthy tour of duty in Afghanistan.

The camp only occupies part of the 800-acre site, which has been fenced in for security.

The Ministry of Defence spent just over £9 million on the camp, besides the amount spent on the urgently needed married quarters. A new 153-house estate was built at Cashfield Farm, Crowhill, Haverfordwest.

The major contractor for the married quarters and camp was the David McLean Group who, throughout construction, worked closely with the Ministry of Defence and the National Park.

The airfield development project was split into two parts: £2 million was for various new building constructions, including a purpose-built operations block equipped with state of the art communication and electronic equipment, while £7 million was spent on refurbishment and upgrading of accommodation, administration offices and some of the hangars. For some six months while the quarters were being refurbished two hangars were used for accommodation. According to some sources they housed rows upon rows of beds and a few pieces of furniture, resembling a refugee acceptance centre.

Four blocks have been converted as female accommodation quarters.

Considerable money has been spent on security as a 4km, 2.4m-high fence has been constructed around the barracks and other sensitive areas. Considerable thought went into putting up the fence as most of it is constructed below the horizon level so as to blend in with the surroundings.

One other new addition to the base is a barn-type building used as a firing range where laser range equipment can be used.

Just like its predecessors 14 Signal Regiment participates in most major events in the county, whether it be a small fête or an official engagement. The military has always encouraged sporting activities and members from the regiment represent their unit in various inter-service sporting events ranging from cricket and canoeing to swimming and athletics. Cawdor Barracks also has eager and successful rugby and soccer teams.

The closure of the airfield was seen by many as the final chapter in aviation history in the county. To many people it was an extremely sad event, not only to those in areas that became dependent on the base but also to those posted to Brawdy during the preceding years, who had decided to stay and settle down in the county.

In 1995 the link between Pembrokeshire and the RAF ended, just as it did with the navy in 1974, but a new link began with the army establishing a military presence in the county for the foreseeable future.

Chapter 7

Brawdy's Humanitarian Role

Brawdy's helicopters were always ready and available to assist in all aspects of humanitarian support, not only in the role of search and rescue but also in medical emergencies and general assistance, especially in bad weather; roles which today are covered by air ambulance and the police helicopter.

This role was maintained by the Fleet Air Arm station helicopter flight from 1955 to 1970, and also by the Royal Air Force D Flight No.22 Squadron and B Flight of No.202 Search and Rescue Squadron, from 1971 to 1995.

The service has always provided a good medical emergency coverage working closely with hospitals, the ambulance service, the police, the fire service and the coast guard.

Service medical officers provided most of the coverage from Monday to Friday, and between 8 a.m. and 6 p.m., but most of the SAR and medical coverage outside these hours was covered by local General Practitioners who gave up their free time at weekends to assist the helicopter crews. One such devoted GP was Dr George Middleton of St David's, who attended about 90 SAR call-outs between 1956 and 1993.

Dr G. Middleton, a civilian, served with both Fleet Air Arm and Royal Air Force, beginning in the cramped conditions of a naval Westland Dragonfly helicopter on 8 December 1956, progressing on to the larger Westland Whirlwind, and eventually to the spacious Westland Sea King, which is the standard SAR helicopter in service today. Dr Middleton was involved in all aspects of SAR call-outs, especially at the weekends, whether it was an emergency medical response where an ambulance could not get to the patient in time or attending to an injured seaman or a ditched pilot.

Although Pembrokeshire benefits from warm Atlantic currents, it is also prone to extremely bad winter weather with drifting snow and prolonged freezing conditions.

The Royal Navy's first search and rescue helicopter was the Westland Dragonfly. (D. Edwards)

Humanitarian aspect of call-outs included delivering of yeast for bread to a baker in Maenclochog during the heavy snowfall of 1953.

A Westland Whirlwind HAR 10 of No.22 Squadron landing near a remote farmstead.

A successful rescue by a Sea King of No.202 Squadron. (Via RAF Brawdy)

A Sea King of B Flight en route to another call-out.

It is during these times that Brawdy helicopters were often called out to assist the emergency services.

A typical example of the role of Brawdy's helicopter call-outs occurred on 8 January 1963 in severe weather, when most of the county was covered with a blanket of snow, with snow drifts ranging between 6ft and 20ft. It took some effort to get the helicopters out of the hangars because of snowdrifts and frozen door runners. During the day Brawdy received several call-outs, such as the distress call from the police in Eglwyswrw regarding a patient who had been diagnosed by a doctor over the phone for a burst appendix. The patient father and some neighbours cleared a landing place for the helicopter and lighted fires when the aircraft approached, as visibility had deteriorated. The Whirlwind, piloted by Lt Sirett and his crew, Lts Marr and Wakefield and Leading Airman Faulcorner, together with Dr Middleton, flew to the remote farm and landed safely, picking up the patient and flying on to Haverfordwest Hospital.

Another call-out came to pick up a man found frozen next to the wall of an unoccupied house at Glasfryn, near Sealyham Cross. Unable to find a suitable area to land, a snowplough cleared a stretch of road and the helicopter was able to touch down and pick up the patient. Within a short time the Whirlwind landed at Rifleman Field, Haverfordwest, and the man was taken by road to hospital.

In the afternoon the helicopter was required by South Wales Electricity Board to convey engineers from Haverfordwest to Solva and St David's to repair power lines. To end up a busy day they picked up a Coast Guard officer from Strumble Head lighthouse, who had been stranded there since the previous day, and needed to be airlifted to Fishguard.

Demanding workloads seemed to occur during extremely bad weather. On 10 January 1982, again during the heavy snow, Dr Middleton was involved in call-outs once more. This time he was away from home for over six hours and covered a distance of well over 100 miles in a Westland Sea King helicopter.

The first call was to deliver baby milk to a remote farmstead cut off by a snowdrift, and then to carry a patient to Withybush Hospital for dialysis treatment. Then they collected a second helicopter aircrew from their home and flew them to the air station.

The helicopter responded to an emergency call for a mother-to-be whose home was cut off by snowdrifts with no electricity and, eventually, no telephone. By the time the Sea King arrived at the farm the baby had been born but needed urgent hospital treatment. With great professionalism the pilot, Flt Lt Malcolm Carlisle, landed the helicopter in the snowdrifts near the farmstead. Dr Middleton was able to accompany the newborn baby and mother to Bronglas Hospital where they made a perfect recovery.

The team answered another emergency from the police to pick up a driver trapped in his car in the vicinity of Plynlimmon. The driver was suffering from hypothermia, as was another victim at Dyffryn Castell whose front door had been blown in by the wind and the house filled with snow. Both were taken to hospital in Aberystwyth.

On the return flight to Brawdy the helicopter landed at the RAE airfield at Aberporth for refuelling, while at the airfield the team was called out to assist the local ambulance service pick up an injured person with a fracture from Lampeter and take him to Cardigan Hospital, whereupon the crew collected two more patients and proceeded to Withybush Hospital at Haverfordwest. Finally, Dr Middleton returned home to St David's late that evening.

Whenever there was a call-out or distress call in the Irish Sea or off the Irish coast Dr Middleton was picked up from St David's rugby field, which gained valuable time, saved from making the journey from St David's to the airfield.

Perhaps one of the longest and most demanding rescue flights conducted by both RAF and RN helicopters was on 20/21 May 1991: an air operation in co-operation with the Irish Guardia in search for the Air India Boeing 747 blown up by terrorists 600 miles off the south-west coast of Ireland. The rescue mission involved the Sea King being refuelled at Cork, and again on the deck of the Royal Fleet Auxiliary ship RFA *Argus*. All 304 passengers and crew of the airliner perished. Sea Kings from Brawdy, Chivenor and RNAS Culdrose, together with surface ships, were involved in the search.

Another rescue mission involving Dr Middleton was the recovery of injured seamen from the submarine HMS *Oracle* some 1,130 miles from Brawdy.

Like the rest of the helicopter crew, Dr Middleton had to attend various courses in rescue procedures, ranging from being lowered by winch to how to survive if the helicopter had to ditch. The courses were held at the search and rescue school at RAF Valley and, according to Dr Middleton, the flight there and back was the most enjoyable one he had ever undertaken, for the helicopter followed the coast to Anglesey.

After nearly forty years of devoted service to SAR at Brawdy, Dr Middleton's last Sea King call-out flight was on 23 September 1993.

During the Admiralty tenure of the airfield the station flight of usually two or three helicopters were available for search and rescue duties. Initially the piston-engined Westland Dragonfly was used, but this was soon replaced by the larger Whirlwind HAS7, then the turbine-powered Westland Whirlwind HAR9.

When the Royal Air Force resumed control of Brawdy in 1971 search and rescue duties were covered by Whirlwinds of D Flight (No.22 Squadron) and were replaced in 1979 by Whirlwinds and Sea Kings of B Flight (No.202 Squadron), which remained at Brawdy until 1995.

The Sea King was equipped with up to date homing systems, satellite navigation and search radar which enabled it to home in on any distress beacons. The standard SAR crew was made up of four members: two pilots, one being the aircraft captain, a radar operator/winch operator at the rescue scene and a winch man, normally trained to paramedic standard.

It is worth noting that B Flight of No.202 squadron had an impressive record. Callouts varied from year to year: the highest was in 1990 when they responded to 170 calls, both military and civilian. In all 169 people were airlifted to safety that year, which was just an average number rescued during the Flight's stay at Brawdy.

Between 1979 and 1996 B Flights was scrambled to well over 2,000 call-outs, ranging from searching for drifting dinghies at sea to missing people on land, or assisting coast guards rescuing people on cliffs, as well as searching for and rescuing downed pilots. The Flight always maintained a fifteen-minute readiness state during daylight hours and a forty-five-minute readiness state during hours of darkness. The squadron was involved in numerous incidents and call-outs which, due to space available, cannot be included here. However, some are worth mentioning, such as the rescue of Greek seamen from a sinking ship in which outstanding bravery earned the helicopter crew gallantry medals from the Greek government. They also received an official acknowledgement from the Italian government for rescuing a downed pilot who ran out of fuel crossing the Atlantic. B Flight has had the honour of being awarded the Edward and Maise Lewis award for saving of lives at sea on a number of occasions. This great honour is awarded annually by the Shipwrecked Mariners Society.

Finally, the Flight was often asked to fly equipment and supplies to Skomer and Skokholm islands on behalf of the Dyfed Wildlife Trust. This became a favourite operation with most crews.

With the closure of Brawdy as an airfield it seems that the search and rescue element has left the county, and with it the humanitarian aspects of the service.

During the redevelopment phase in 1995 a B Flight crew room was demolished and with it decades of outstanding bravery from the helicopter crews.

Chapter 8

Brawdy's Air Displays

Brawdy has attracted people for decades from near and far to its annual air displays, which had became renowned throughout South Wales. It gave people an opportunity to not only witness wonderful displays but also see at close quarters the modern equipment used by the armed services.

The first air display, or naval air day, as it was then called, was held at Brawdy by the Fleet Air Arm in August 1953. The display was held at a time when British forces were involved in the Korean War and operating against insurgents in Malaya.

In the immediate post-war period the RAF and naval air service strength was at its minimum, while slowly jet aircraft was replacing the piston engine types, so air displays became an exciting event for the onlookers.

It was only on 20 May 1953 that the Naval Air Service was officially renamed the Fleet Air Arm and its aircraft appeared in their new livery.

To be certain of success the Fleet Air Arm made sure the event was well publicised with posters, adverts in local papers and pamphlets distributed through village post offices, shops and halls throughout the county.

The air display attracted visitors from all over the county: pre-display publicity had done the trick. Even local bus companies organised day trips from Cardigan, Crymych, Maenclochog in the north, Tenby, Saundersfoot, Pembroke and Haverfordwest in the south. The early 1950s was a time when private cars were very few and people relied on public transport.

The display was opened by a fly-past of aircraft towing a banner reading 'Welcome to Brawdy', which became the standard FAA opening theme.

Aircraft on display, both static and in the air, included the Douglas Skyraider AEW 1s of No.849 Squadron, which was reformed at Brawdy in July 1952. There were also displays by Supermarine Attackers, Sea Hornets, Mosquitoes and Meteor T7s of the Fleet Requirement Unit, followed by a mass take off by Hawker Sea Fury FB2s of No.807 Squadron. The spectators were treated to a scramble followed by a spectacle formation of Hawker Sea Hawk F1s of No.806 Squadron, and formation aerobatics by Sea Vampires. There was a helicopter rescue demonstration performed by the FAA Dragonflies of the search and rescue flight. The station flight, comprising Vampires and Meteors, made a mock attack, with explosions, on vehicles parked at the far end of the airfield.

The Royal Air Force also contributed to the display with a Handley Page Hastings C1 of RAF Transport Command, a Bristol Sycamore helicopter, RAF parachutists, Vampires and a Tempest TT of No.233 OCU at Pembrey. Crowds witnessed the agility of the Hawker Hunter of fighter command, which gave a breathtaking demonstration, followed by a fly-past of two Sunderland GR5 flying boats from No.235 Operational Conversion Unit, Pembroke Dock.

A typical naval air day programme from 1959.

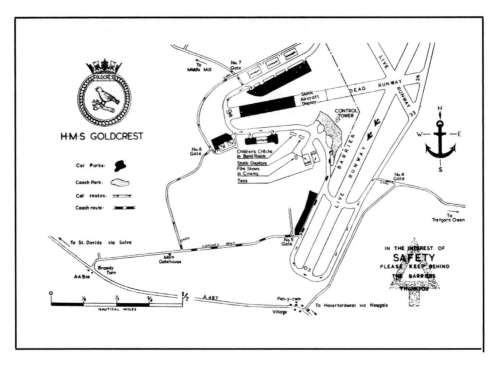

Plan of the display area during the 1959 air day.

Three DH Vampire T22 trainers of No.727 Naval Squadron giving a formation aerobatic display. (D. Edwards)

Fly-past by naval aircraft. In the photograph can be seen Sea Hawks, Sea Venoms, Vampires and Sea Balliols.

Even in 1953 there was some congestion on the narrow country roads around Pen y Cwm, Newgale and Solva, a foretaste of the congestion that would occur in later years as the air display became more popular and cars became more common.

The 1954 display involved a high speed welcome from two Gloster Meteors, which startled the spectators, followed with an aerobatics display by Sea Venoms of No. 890 Squadron, and perhaps one of the most spectacular sights: a stream take off of forty-eight aircraft belonging to Nos 719, 801, 814, 826 and 831 Naval Air Squadrons. Also that year Pembrokeshire spectators were introduced to the RAF Canadair-built North American F86E Sabre. The RAF received 460 Sabres, all of which were delivered in 1952. The Sabres were a much needed stop-gap fighter capable of supersonic speed until the delivery of the Hawker Hunter. During the show a Sabre attempted to break the sound barrier, something which would not be tolerated today. According to some sources a double bang was heard over St Brides Bay, although officially it was denied, stating that the aircraft was some 10mph short of the speed of sound.

In the 1956 the crowds were thrilled by the newly formed RAF 'Black Arrows' of Treble One (No. 111) Squadron, Hawker Hunter F6s painted black. The team visited Brawdy on four occasions. During the 1959 air display the county was deafened by the roar of the RAF V-Bomber the Avro Vulcan showing off its pace over the airfield.

Two ratings staring in disbelief as Balliol WL726 crashes in a plume of black smoke during the air display on 4 August 1956. (D. Edwards)

One of the static aircraft on display during the 1956 air display was a Sea Hawk FGA6 of No.806 Ace of Diamonds Squadron.

The 1957 station display team Hawker Sea Hawks of No.738 Squadron. (Via HMS Goldcrest)

Not all of Brawdy's displays enjoyed good weather. Here we can see a Supermarine Scimitar F1 of the station's maintenance test pilot's school parked on a wet apron. (J. James)

Brawdy's air display was a popular annual event attracting crowds from all over South Wales.

A vintage Fairey Swordfish always attracted a lot of attention from spectators.

A Folland Gnat trainer of the Red Arrows landing at Brawdy after a display.

Other visitors included various Continental aerobatic teams. The photograph shows two Aermacchi MB339 of the Italian Air Force's 'Frecce Tricolori' aerobatic team. (J. James)

In 1990 crowds were drawn to the replica of Alcock's and Brown's Vickers Vimy aircraft that flew the Atlantic non-stop on 14/15 June 1919. (J. James)

One of the largest aircraft to visit Brawdy was the RAF Lockheed Tristar, which attracted a great deal of interest.

BAe Lightnings were always a favourite with the crowds. (J. James)

A Phantom F4 landing after a spectacular solo display.

A line up of various aircraft that took part in the display. A Jaguar, Buccaneer, two F18 Hornets, a Phantom and two F16s. (J. James)

United States Forces aircraft were regular visitors to Brawdy's air displays. This photograph shows a USN F18 Hornet being prepared for flight.

A regular visitor to Brawdy's air displays was the de Havilland Mosquito (RR299) HT-E.

Spectators enthralled by a Westland Wessex helicopter display. (J. James)

The BAe Harrier Jump Jet was another favourite at Brawdy air displays.

No display could be concluded without the Red Arrows aerobatic display team.

The naval air days at Brawdy went from strength to strength, with a vast array of aircraft not only from the FAA and the RAF but also from other NATO countries.

In the sixties spectators were given an opportunity to see new aircraft entering service with the Fleet Air Arm, like the navy's first supersonic fighter, the Supermarine Scimitar F1, and the unusually shaped de Havilland Sea Vixen. There was the turbine-powered Westland Whirlwind helicopter and the various marks of the anti-submarine Fairey Gannet of No.849 Squadron, based at the air station. Visiting aircraft continued to thrill the crowds, especially RAF Lightnings, which always deafened the whole airfield followed by a weary silence while the spectators got their breaths back. Always a solo, Lightning would end its display by a fast run over the airfield and then at the end of the runway would put on its reheat and climb straight up until the onlookers could see only a small dot in the sky. The British Aircraft Corporation Lightning was the only aircraft at the time to have a rate of climb of 50,000ft per minute.

In 1968 the spectators were thrilled by the FAA's own aerobatic display team, 'Simon Sircus', with DH Sea Vixen FAW2s of No.892 Squadron.

The last naval air day took place in 1969 at a time when the FAA carrier force had been reduced and decommissioned.

A trade mark of the Red Arrows display team was the arrow fromation.

RAF Lockheed Tristar K1 of No. 214 Squadron flying over the airfield during the 1986 air display.

However, by 1969 several new aircraft had entered service with the FAA, and these became the star attractions at future displays. In 1968/69 the FAA took delivery of the American McDonnell F4M Phantom and the Blackburn Buccaneer S1, both of which saw service aboard HMS *Ark Royal* in 1962. The first naval operational squadron to be equipped with the Buccaneer was No.801 in January 1963.

As usual there was still a vast array of visiting aircraft provided by the RAF, the United States Air Force and other NATO forces.

The last FAA training flight from Brawdy took place on 1 December 1970, and by the following year the airfield had been handed over to the Department of Environment to oversee care and maintenance.

The Royal Air Force resumed control of the airfield in 1974 but the annual air displays did not resume until 1975.

The first RAF display was outstanding. They clearly intended to show that they were as capable of putting on a good display as the navy.

The instructors of the resident Hunters of No.229 OCU put on a breathtaking display as well as the usual mock air attack on a fort. A Westland Whirlwind of No.22 Squadron demonstrated the art of air sea rescue.

There were the usual solo flights by station flight aircraft, the RAF parachute display team and various aerobatic display teams, concluding with the official RAF aerobatic team.

As usual there were complaints from local residents. One complained that he could not watch his television on a Saturday afternoon because the aircraft affected the transmission. One farmer complained that the noise had a terrible effect on his livestock, and yet the same farmer charged visitors a pound to park in one of his fields near the display.

Within a few years the RAF air days at Brawdy had gained the popularity of the FAA naval air days of the 1950s and '60s, and with success came a larger crowd causing twice the traffic congestion as that of the 1950s.

Throughout the eighties the show attendance record was broken every year. In 1981 attendance to the airfield was put at about 11,000, growing to 15,500 in 1986, and reaching nearly 18,000 by the end of the decade.

In the 1970s there were new aircraft entering service with the armed forces, such as the Anglo French Jaguar, the American Phantom, the RAF Buccaneer, the Wessex helicopter (replacing the Whirlwind), the BAe VC10 and the Harrier, which was capable of vertical take-offs, becoming a firm favourite with the crowds. By the early eighties Harrier had made several appearances at Brawdy, the first being in 1975.

Vintage aircraft were also a favourite part of the display with many spectators.

During the navy days the Fairey Swordfish had a place of honour in the display, which I remember stirred up memories for a person standing next to me who had made the daring attack on the German battleship *Bismark* in May 1941 from the aircraft carrier HMS *Victorious*.

The Battle of Britain flight with its Lancaster bomber, Spitfire and Hurricane brought back memories to many. The Tiger Moth and the Mosquito (code HT) also took the crowd back to the war years when both were seen at Brawdy.

By the 1980s contribution by NATO air forces had increased; there were aircraft in static display and in the air. One witnessed German Air Force F104 Starfighters, Belgian Air Force Mirages, French Air Force Mirages and Jaguar and the USAF Phantoms, F111 bombers, F16 and F18s. In June 1987 a RAF Lockheed Tristar landed at Brawdy, up to then the heaviest aircraft to land on Pembrokeshire soil.

All the RAF aerobatic display teams have visited Bawdy during its air days. The first was No.111 squadron Black Arrow team with its Hunter F6s, which perhaps was the first true formation display team. The Black Arrow team was the official display team from 1956 to 1960, and was replaced for two years by sixteen Hunters of No.92 Squadron, known as Blue Diamonds. Also during 1961/62, No.74 Squadron, equipped with Lightings (Flying Tigers), started making appearances at air displays. The most famous of the Lightning formation teams were the Firebirds of No.56 Squadron with nine aircraft. This team made several visits to the Brawdy air displays. The Lighting was not the ideal aircraft for formation flying, but in the hands of skilled pilots it proved to be a show puller.

The official RAF display team from 1965 was the Red Arrows, comprising of aircraft from the Flying Training School. Initially, the aircraft were the red painted Folland Gnat T1s, but the Gnats were phased out and replaced by the BAe Hawk T1/1A.

Although by the 1980s the date of the RAF air days varied from year to year to fit in with RAF commitments, other displays and 'at home' events were held throughout RAF airfields in the UK. However, all the Brawdy displays were held during the summer months – which did not prevent some extremely wet ones.

One notable event worth mentioning occurred on 25 July 1984 when a Hunter XE624, piloted by No.234 Squadron's commanding officer, Squadron Leader 'Gus' Crockett, flew the aircraft's last sortie. After completing a fifteen-minute flight, XE624 had accumulated 5,714 air-hours since leaving the production line in June 1956. The following year the aircraft had a place of honour as the stations gate guardian.

When all flying training ceased at Brawdy in August 1992, the last air display was held in July 1991, and attracted a record number of visitors as well as a record number of exhibits and aircraft from both the British armed forces and NATO forces.

During the thirty years or so of the air displays at Brawdy only two major accidents ending in fatalities occurred. Strangely, the two tragedies happened thirty years apart, nearly to the exact date.

The first of the tragedies occurred during the naval air day on 4 August 1956, in which a Boulton Paul Sea Balliol (WL726) belonging to No.727 Squadron crashed during a solo display. In front of over 10,000 spectators the pilot, Lt John Mark Mitchell, a twenty-three year old from Liss in Hampshire, gave a breathtaking solo display. The author was unfortunate enough to be present and witnessed the accident.

It seemed that Lt Mitchell climbed his Rolls Royce Merlin-powered Balliol trainer to a certain height, then switched off the engine to dive, restarting his engine and pulling out of the dive at the last minute. On his second attempt the engine failed to re-start and the aircraft disappeared behind a slight dip on the edge of the airfield. All the spectators could see was a black plume of smoke rising from the area (see page 88, top photo).

The display continued with the next event in the programme being an aerobatic display by a solo Sea Hawk, which took the spectators' thoughts off the black smoke.

At the end of the display the crowd disappeared without knowing the true extent of the accident they had witnessed. It was not until people got home that they heard on the news that a pilot had died in the crash.

On the following Monday an inquest was held at Haverfordwest into the tragedy, which recorded a verdict of accidental death as the result of a misjudged aerobatic manoeuvre.

The three ratings, Leading Airman Gerald Cluett, Naval Airman Peter Parker and Donald Bird, who were on duty near the spot, and who tried in vain to rescue Lt Mitchell, were presented with an illuminated scroll by Brawdy's commanding officer, Captain Frank Stovin-Bradford DSC, in recognition of their brave efforts.

The United States Air Force and Naval Service had always participated in Brawdy's air days. However, during the air display on 24 July 1986, in front of yet another record-breaking crowd of nearly 15,000, the second tragedy occurred. Spectators were once again thrilled by a number of United States Air Force aircraft including the F111 and the McDonnell RF4C Phantom belonging to the 10th Tactical Reconnaissance Wing based at RAF Alconbury, Cambridgeshire.

The Phantom flown by pilot Captain Mark Makowski of Wilmington, Delaware, and weapon systems operator 2nd Lt Dewayne Danielson of Pleasanton, California, made several low and high-speed passes over the airfield, pulling out over the sea.

Eyewitnesses at the display, and those watching the spectacle from Newgale beach, reported that the Phantom seemed to climb after making a fast low-level pass over the airfield, but the aircraft then seemed to loose power and fell back into the sea. Some of the spectators reported seeing something fall off the aircraft when it went into ascent.

It seemed that the crew knew something was wrong and tried to eject, but were too low for the ejector seat to have an effect.

A Sea King search and rescue plane of B Flight (No.202 Squadron) was despatched within minutes of the crash, but it took another hour to recover the bodies from the sea.

After a thorough investigation by USAF and the RAF crash investigation teams the accident was blamed on a low-level stall and the failure of the J79 engine reheats to ignite. Initially it was thought that a bird could be responsible, but after recovering the aircraft this was ruled out.

Thankfully, major accidents were very rare at Brawdy, although there were several minor ones such as incidents in which a member of the free falling parachute display team broke his ankle on landing, a pilot slipped on oil and the occasional bursting tyre – all events thta were never revealed to the public.

Throughout the years the air displays turned out to provide ideal public relations for both Royal Navy and the Royal Air Force. It gave the people of Pembrokeshire and beyond an opportunity to meet the services, to be guests of the military for the day and see for themselves the equipment that was part of the country's defence, and which, as tax payers, they had helped acquire.

Chapter 9

United States Navy Facilities

The United States Navy oceanographic research station was situated just off the approach road to the main entrance of the airfield, coming from the A487. Officially the research station existence was always denied, but it was known that it was a processing centre for a network of underwater microphones and sensors situated off the British Isles and in the Atlantic for listening to Soviet submarine movements in the ocean.

Its existence was kept secret, and on several occasions journalists intending to write about the base were threatened with the Official Secrets Act. The only articles that seemed to get the clearance were those which came up with outrageous and out of this world explanations.

The base was mentioned in fairly great detail in the book by Peter Paget, *The Welsh Triangle*, as it seems that Brawdy and the surrounding area was a centre for UFO sightings. When the USN left and the base was converted for use as a business park none of the secret underground facilities mentioned in this book were ever found.

Secret bases have always been centres of speculation and mystery, and have provided authors with an endless stream of myth and interest. When the airfield closed and the secret base was declassified, in 1995, information became readily available.

SOSUS (Sound Surveillance System United States), or Project Caesar, as it was known, began in 1954 to track and trace Soviet submarines in the Atlantic. The growing Soviet submarine fleet was a great concern to NATO, and especially the United States. The USN was authorised to build several SOSUS stations in Europe to track Soviet submarine movements in the North Atlantic.

The base at Brawdy was completed and opened in 1973. The 7.6-acre NAVFAC (Naval Facility) consisted of a 58,000sq.ft terminal building, the operation block, office and admin block, the workshop, garages and even its own generator. Although it was

Navfac base, 1979. (Via USN)

Navfac base at Brawdy in the nineties. (Via USN)

self-contained the USN personnel were billeted in a newly built accommodation block on the main site.

The intelligence facility was manned by twenty-two USN officers and 278 other ranks. Numbers of staff varied considerably during this period as they were constantly being moved between SOSUS bases. As a NATO member and host country the RAF and RN had their liaison staff permanently based at the facility.

It seems that over $20 million was spent on the base at Brawdy between 1978 and 1984. Nearly 80 per cent of the budget was allocated to electronic and computer equipment. The amount spent on updates and modification is not known, although $3.6 million covered an extension to the terminal block in 1981.

The terminal building, or main operation room, had a series of heavy metal doors with an air lock in between each one. Just inside the outer door was a guardroom with bulletproof glass. The building was split into two floors or, in naval terms, two decks. On the ground floor was the main computer and electronic equipment, as well as the recreation section for the staff and a storeroom. On the second deck was the captain's residence, special lounges with their own kitchen, offices and accommodation for RAF and RN liaison teams, as well as various classrooms. The whole building was air conditioned and had a humidity control. The main ops room was surrounded by sound dampers and was protected against electromagnetic snoopers. The terminal was blast proof, and could withstand almost anything except a direct hit. It was also built to withstand nuclear or biological fallout.

On top of the ops room was a guard tower with all-round visibility.

The base had its own generator, which produced all the electricity needed as well as all providing hot water for heating and washing. So as not to be a burden on the local supply, an underwater tank was built for water storage. A detail of the base and buildings layout was obtained in 2002 when the base was put up for sale or lease, and the author was privileged enough to visit.

The base security was the responsibility of the US Marine Corp security force, the 13th Atlantic Division, who were more or less the last personnel to depart from Brawdy.

Over the years a number of articles have been written about the base, mostly in the States. One such report suggested that, because of the shape of St Brides Bay, that several hydrophones had been placed at various intervals to catch the sound of the submarines out to sea. This is doubtful as the bay faces Ireland, which would block any sound.

However, one report of interest was eventually released by the USN: up to 1993 very little had been known about the base and much of that was speculation, until it was revealed that a scientific researcher studying whale movements obtained recordings of whale song from the Brawdy base. It seems that the naval technicians had tracked the same whale for forty days, from Iceland to Bermuda. This gave military writers some idea of the sensitivity of the equipment at the base. After all, a Soviet submarine is much noisier than a whale.

Considering that the United States and the United Kingdom were partners in NATO, relations between the RAF base and NAVFAC were not always good, especially between off-duty personnel. On a number of occasions military police were called to sort out arguments in the NAAFI, and civilian police to the local pubs.

NAVFAC came under RAF station bylaws, as is normal for a foreign base on British soil, and therefore all emergencies would be under the jurisdiction of the RAF. However, a fire occurred at NAVFAC and the fire alarm went off at RAF Brawdy. A RAF fire control team raced over to the base but was told at gunpoint that they did not have permission to enter. As one fireman said at the time, 'Next time they can roast as far I am concerned'. As time went by a closer relationship developed between the RAF and the USN.

Throughout its existence the base was subjected to several anti-nuclear protest actions, as most protesters thought that it was a UN nuclear weapon storage facility. The biggest demonstration was in 1982 when 'Women for Life on Earth' descended on Brawdy. The march began at Cardiff with women from Greenham Common forming the nucleus of the demonstration. By the time it reached Pembrokeshire thousands more women and children had joined the march. The demonstration was not just an annoyance to the base and RAF Brawdy but to local people and local villages whose daily lives were disrupted.

With the prospect of the airfield closing, the USN closed the base on 1 October 1995 and its functions were transferred to a new establishment at RAF St Mawgan in Cornwall.

Most of the sensitive equipment was flown out in USAF Lockheed Galaxy transport aircraft, which, as you may recall, were the heaviest aircraft to land in Pembrokeshire. Special computer experts from the States were flown into Brawdy to dismantle and remove all electronic equipment. To the amazement of the RAF personnel, the equipment was transferred from the facility to the awaiting transport under armed US Marine guard. No other personnel were allowed within 100 yards of the aircraft, not even the fire tender.

After the computers were removed every corner was double-searched in case some valuable document had been mislaid. According to sources fifty ratings spent a whole week going through the building after everything had been moved. Most of the furniture fittings that were not removed by navy technicians were auctioned off.

Today all the buildings are intact and the base forms part of the Brawdy Business Park.

At the time of writing several companies have already moved in, or are about to move in, to this exceptionally interesting setting. The terminal block has been renamed St David's House.

Chapter 10

Summary of Squadrons, Units and Aircraft based in Brawdy

ROYAL AIR FORCE

Sqd	Code	Aircraft Type	Based at
1944–1947			
53	FH	Liberator VI, VIII	St David's
58	GE	HP Halifax GR 2	St David's and Brawdy
206	VX	Fortress I and II	St David's
220	NR	Fortress II, Liberator V, VI, VIII	St David's
502	V9	HP Halifax GR2	St David's
517	X9	Halifax III (Met) Hampden V	
		Hudson II, Fortress I, Stirling Met 4	Brawdy
517	X9	Halifax III (Met)	St David's
521	5O	Halifax III and V	
595	7B	Martinet, Spitfire	Oxford, Hewley
8OTU	BE	Spitfire IX, PR 9, Mosquito	

Note: squadrons based at St David's also used Brawdy for refuelling and storage.

1974-1998

22 D Flight	Westland Whirlwind
63	Hawker Hunter F6, T7
	Jet Provost T4, BAe Hawk T1A
79	Hawker Hunter FGA 9, FR 10, T7, Meteor T7, TT8
234	Hawker Hunter F6, T7
202 B Flight	Westland Sea King HAR3

Other Units

229 OCU	Hawker Hunter T8, Hawk T1A
	(Comprising Nos 63, 79 and 234, re-numbered No. TWU)

NAVAL SQUADRONS BASED AT BRAWDY
Fleet Air Arm

1946-1974

ASR Flight	Westland Dragonfly, Whirlwind HAR10, HS7
727	Sea Balliol T21, Sea Prince, Sea Vampire T22
736	Supermarine Scimitar F1
738	Sea Hawks (various marks)
738	Hawker Hunter T8, GA11
748	Hellcats 11NF, Harvard II, Firefly
751	Avenger AS4, DH Sea Venom
759	Percival Proctor, Miles Master II
759	Miles Martinet TT1, Hunter T8, T8C
784	Hellcat IINF, Harvard I, Firefly 4
787	Supermarine Attacker FB1
800	Hawker Sea Hawks F1, F2, FGA4 and 6
801	Hawker Sea Hawks F1, F2, FGA4 and 6
802	Hawker Sea Fury FB III
804	Hawker Sea Fury FB III, Sea Hawks FGA6
806	Hawker Sea Hawk F1, F2
807	Hawker Sea Hawk F1, FGA 6
811	DH Sea Mosquito T33
813	Westland Wyvern S4
821	Fairey Seal (land version)
824	Fairey Gannet AS1
831 (BY)	DH Sea Venom, Hunting Sea Prince
849 (BY)	Douglas Skyraider AEW1, Fairey Gannet AS4, Gannet AEW3, COD4, T5

891	DH Sea Venom FAW21
892	DH Sea Vixen FAW2
893	DH Sea Venom FAW21
895	Sea Hawks FGA4 and 6
898	Sea Hawk F2
1831 (BY)	Sea Balliol, Sea Vampire, Attacker F2, FB1
FRU	Sea Hornet F1, Sea Mosquito T33, Meteor T7
	Attacker F1, based at St David's and Brawdy
VS6 USN	PBY Catalina

Appendix I

Station Badges, Royal Navy Period 1946–1971

HMS Goldcrest, RN Period 1946–1971

On 1 January 1946 Brawdy Airfield was transferred to Admiralty control as a naval air station and, as was traditional with the Royal Navy, all bases were classed as ships and given a name. Brawdy became known as HMS Goldcrest II, a classification that indicated its status as a satellite airfield to HMS Goldcrest I at Dale. RNAS Dale was officially closed on 13 December 1947, and Brawdy was re-commissioned on 4 September 1952 as HMS Goldcrest. Therefore, the naval air station was awarded its own badge featuring a goldcrest perched on a branch (representing a resting-place for the bird after a flight).

The goldcrest is the common name for one of the smallest birds in the British Isles. The bird's back is moss green in colour, while its underside is a pale olive or buff. Its most striking feature is the orange crown of the males, which is bounded with yellow and black. It is a very active bird, which accurately represented the business of the air station.

Station Badge, RAF Period 1984–1992

In 1984 RAF Brawdy was awarded a new badge, or crest, which depicted a sea dragon with one claw touching the feathers of the Prince of Wales, who was the Honorary Air Commodore of the station. The other claw was clasping the sword of strike command. The sea dragon's upper torso was painted red, representing the red dragon of Wales, while the lower body was azure blue, representing Brawdy's proximity to the sea during the Second World War and its association with the Fleet Air Arm, 1946–1974. The station's Welsh motto was 'Amddiffynfa y Gorllewin', which translates to 'Stronghold in the West'.

It is worth noting that a similar sea dragon appears on the Preseli District Council coat of arms.

HMS Goldcrest. (Via HMS Goldcrest)

RAF Brawdy's station badge. (Via RAF Brawdy)

Appendix II

Commanding Officers of Royal Naval Air Station Brawdy

August 1952–July 1954	Captain R.E.N. Kearney OBE, RN
July 1954–July 1956	Captain D.C.E.F. Gibson DSC, RN
August 1956–September 1958	Captain F. Stovin-Bradford DSC, RN
October 1958–July 1959	Captain H.R.B. Janvrin DSC, RN
July 1959–August 1961	Captain E.S. Carver DSC, RN
August 1961–January 1963	Commander P.R.S. Bravn MBE, RN
January 1963–February 1965	Captain W.I. Campbell, RN
February 1965–March 1967	Captain P.M. Austin, RN
March 1967–May 1969	Captain A.B.B. Clark, RN
May 1969–December 1970	Captain R.L. Eveleigh DSC, RN
December 1970–March 1971	Commander P.B. Cowan, RN

Appendix III

Brawdy's Gate Guardian

Since the Second World War it has been Royal Air Force policy to have a static aircraft parked next to the main gates of airfields, maintenance depots and headquarters. These static displays are known as gate guardians and over the years the Fleet Air Arm and the Army Air Corps have adopted the idea.

Aircraft and helicopters used were the types operated on that particular base. In the post-war period the Spitfire became a favourite with most camps, gradually being replaced by more modern popular aircraft.

During Fleet Air Arm control several types of aircraft appeared at different times as gate guardians, including a Vampire, a Sea Hawk, a Gannet and eventually a Hawker Hunter in No.738 Squadron's RN livery. Perhaps the most stunning, and the most confusing to air spotters, was Sea Hawk XE340 with its dual markings. On its starboard side it carried the livery of No.806 Squadron, Ace of Diamonds. When the FAA left the Sea Hawk was removed to RNAS Lossiemouth. Today XE340 is one of the exhibits at the Montrose Air Station heritage centre.

The most popular static display was the Supermarine Spitfire and, like most RAF airfields, Brawdy displayed a Supermarine Spitfire (PRXIX - PS915). But, because of its remarkable condition, the RR Griffon-powered Spitfire was later removed from Brawdy and put in storage. After hundreds of man-hours the Spitfire was restored to flying condition and today flies as part of the RAF Battle of Britain Memorial Flight.

When the Royal Air Force resumed control of the airfield a Hawker Hunter FGA9 (XE624) became the new gate guardian, and remained at her post until the airfield closed.

The Hunter (XE624) had a distinguished career: it first flew on 17 June 1956, and was delivered to No.263 Squadron. In 1959 it joined No.1 Squadron at RAF Wattisham

The Sea Hawk XX340 was unique as it appeared with the Ace of Diamonds emblem on one side and the Flying Fish on the other. It continued to fly in air displays until it became the gate guardian. (Air Heritage)

where it remained until March 1960, when it was returned to the manufacturer to be converted into a FGA9. The Hunter was re-issued to No.1 Squadron at West Raynham in November 1963, and was finally delivered to No.229 OCU at Chivenor in September 1970. It reached TWU at Brawdy in March 1975 with No.234 Squadron.

The aircraft's last sortie was on 25 July 1984 and it was eventually retired after completing twenty-eight years' service. As a tribute to the type it was decided that it should have a place of honour as the gate guardian. For a number of years the aircraft was kept in pristine condition by the 1st Rock Beaver Colony.

In the eighties a number of the gate guardians throughout the RAF were in a poor state of repair, and many were replaced by fibreglass replicas, while the originals were transferred to various museums, including the RAF Museum at Hendon.

Hawker Sea Hawk (XX340), gate guardian of No.806 Ace of Diamonds Squadron.

Hawker Sea Hawk (XX340) with No.898 Squadron's flying fish markings (1968).

Supermarine Spitfire PRXIX (PS915). (Via MAP)

Hawker Hunter FGA 9 (XE624).

Hawker Hunter 8565M of No.43 Squadron was the gate guardian in 1980. (Air Heritage)

Appendix IV

Certain Royal Navy Squadrons Associated with Brawdy

No.806 Naval Air Squadron, Ace of Diamonds

No.806 Squadron was formed at Eastleigh on 15 February 1940, equipped with eight Blackburn Skuas and four Roc aircraft. After three months of intensive training the unit was involved in attacking enemy shipping and oil storage tanks in occupied Bergen, Norway.

On 15 July 1940 the squadron was re-equipped with the standard naval fighter, the Fairey Fulmar. The squadron, with its twelve aircraft, embarked in the aircraft carrier HMS *Illustrious* in August, and for the next year saw action in the Mediterranean theatre. While escorting the Malta convoys the squadron was accredited with twenty-three enemy aircraft shot down.

In many respects the Fulmer was inferior to most enemy fighters so was replaced by the Sea Hurricane in the autumn of 1941. The squadron also flew from HMS *Formidable* in support of land forces in the Western desert.

For a brief period in January 1942 No.806 was once again re-equipped with twelve Fulmars, which operated from Ceylon and from the carriers *Indomitable* and *Illustrious*, in defence of Ceylon, Diego Suarez and Madagascar.

HMS *Illustrious*, along with half the squadron, returned to the Mediterranean for the reinforcement operation of Malta, and by the end of the year was disbanded, while the other half remained in the Far East before being amalgamated with No.803 at Tonga in 1943.

The squadron was reformed on 1 August 1945 at Macrihanish with twenty-five Supermarine Seafire Mk III and XVs and twelve Mk XVs, and embarked aboard HMS *Glory* in May 1946.

The squadron was disbanded again in the early '50s, leaving a gap in the naval air defence. However, on 2 March 1953 No.806 Squadron was reformed at RNAS Brawdy with the Hawker Sea Hawk F1, making them the first Seahawk squadron in the Fleet Air Arm.

It was at this time that the squadron adopted the Ace of Diamonds card symbol on their aircraft. It remained at Brawdy until 5 February 1954, where most of the conversion was done before embarking on a naval carrier. After a brief period aboard Royal Navy aircraft carriers the unit was disbanded within two years.

On 14 January 1957 No.806 Squadron was reformed at Brawdy with Sea Hawks F2 and FGA4s. The commissioning service was attended by Rear Admiral Charles Evans, who commanded the unit when it was first formed at Eastleigh in 1940. Rear Admiral Evans eventually became a Vice Admiral. For the next few years the squadron operated from the aircraft carrier HMS *Eagle* in the Middle East and the Mediterranean area, as well as other naval air stations in the UK.

In 1959 the squadron made a brief visit to Brawdy for re-equipping and preparation for another overseas deployment. In October 1959 the squadron embarked again on HMS *Eagle* for a tour of duty in the Far East. It is worth noting that while at Brawdy they formed a highly co-ordinated formation aerobatic team, flying as the Ace of Diamonds. This was the squadron's last visit to Pembrokeshire.

No.849 Squadron

No.849 Squadron was another naval squadron that was more or less permanently based at Brawdy. The squadron was reformed at Brawdy in 1959, equipped with ex-No.778 Douglas Sky Raider AEW1s, an airborne early warning variant of the USN fighter-bomber. The Fleet Air Arm version had a crew of three with a radar dome under the fuselage and provision for under-wing armaments. This type equipped two squadrons until being replaced by the Fairey Gannet AEW in 1960. The AEW version, with its dorsal radar dome, was affectionately known by Brawdy personnel as the 'pregnant Gannet'.

Elements of the squadron served on RN aircraft carriers while the rest remained at Brawdy, used for training. However, while at RNAS Culdrose the squadron was re-equipped with the new Fairey Gannet.

No.849 Squadron returned to Brawdy on 15 December 1964, equipped with four versions of the Fairey Gannet. The AEW3 version was fitted with an AN/APS radar dome under the fuselage (a radar removed from the Skyraiders), the AS4 for anti-submarine duties and the COD4 for fleet transport between the carriers and shore bases. This latter version could carry two passengers in the aft seats, along with mail and essential equipment in special racks in the bomb bay. The T5 was a training version, enabling crews to carry out anti-submarine work, operating radars and weapon use. Torpedo and depth charge exercises were carried out in Cardigan Bay.

Brawdy's involvement served two functions: supplying an operational element to the fleet and fulfilling the squadron's training role.

Hawker Sea Hawk of No.806 Squadron Ace of Diamonds.

Fairey Gannet AS4 of No.849 Squadron Royal Navy.

Fairey Gannet AEW of No.849 Squadron.

Hawker Hunter FGA9 of No.234 Squadron in 1982.

BAe Hawk T1 of No.1 Tactical Weapons Unit landing in 1990. Note the 30mm Aden gun pod underneath.

No.849 was divided into five flights, with Headquarters based at Brawdy, and A, B, C, and D Flights deployed on Royal Navy aircraft carriers. All were based at Brawdy between deployments.

A Flight was deployed on HMS *Victorious*, B Flight on HMS *Centaur*, C Flight on HMS *Ark Royal* and D Flight on HMS *Eagle*. These flights remained on the individual carriers until they were decommissioned.

Each carrier flight consisted of four AEW3, four AS1 and one COD4, while Brawdy (HQ) flight consisted of three or four AEWs, three ASs, two COD and five T5, plus reserve aircraft.

In 1970 the naval carrier force was drastically reduced, so by September only two flights remained, B and D Flights, which operated the AEW version on HMS *Ark Royal* and *Eagle*, as well as the HQ Flight based at Brawdy.

A few of the surplus Gannets were painted black and converted for electronic countermeasure training, and remained at Brawdy.

No.849 Squadron left HMS Goldcrest on 19 November 1970 for RNAS Culdrose, but eventually moved to RNAS Lossiemouth in Scotland where they remained until being disbanded on 15 December 1978. Only the AEW version remained in service as the other anti-submarine duties were taken over by the naval helicopter element.

D Flight was deployed aboard HMS *Eagle* until January 1972 when the carrier was decommissioned, leaving HQ Flight at Lossimouth and B Flight aboard the carrier HMS *Ark Royal*, which remained in service until December 1978 when it too was decommissioned. No.849 Squadron was eventually disbanded on 15 December 1978, and the Gannets were retired from service, although the early warning radars were used by early warning versions of the Shakleton maritime reconnaissance aircraft.

No.79 Squadron badge.

No.234 Squadron badge.

No.1 TWU Badge

Appendix V

Squadrons that made up No.229 OCU, No.1 TWU, No.63 Squadron and No.229 OCU

No.63 Squadron

No.63 Squadron's history goes back to 5 July 1916 when the Royal Flying Corp squadron was formed at Stirling in Scotland. It was intended as a day bomber unit, equipped with DH4s, for the Western Front, but before it was posted it was diverted to Mesopotamia. The squadron arrived at Basra on 13 August but was not immediately declared operational as most of its personnel were ill.

Eventually the squadron was assigned to the 1st Indian Army to aid their advance up the River Tigris, resulting in the capture of 4,000 Turks at Khan Baghidi, culminating in the surrender of the Turkish Army at Sharqat.

No.63 Squadron was disbanded at Baghdad on 29 February 1920, then reformed in February 1937 at RAF Andover, and equipped with Hawker Hinds and, later, Audax, until it received Fairey Battles in May 1937.

The squadron was designated a training unit on 17 March 1939, and was merged with No.52 Squadron forming No.12 OCU at Benson.

The squadron was reformed on 15 June 1942 and equipped with NA Mustangs for tactical reconnaissance in co-operation with the Army. In March 1944 the unit received Hawker Hurricanes, but was re-equipped with Spitfires within two months.

The squadron's Spitfires provided valuable reconnaissance to naval ships throughout the D-Day landings, and afterwards in Holland. In January 1945 the squadron was disbanded once again, and its aircraft were transferred to No.41 OTU.

Once again the squadron was reactivated on 1 September 1946 with Spitfire XVIs at Middle Wallop, but moved to Thorney Island in December 1947.

In 1948 the squadron received its first jet fighter, the Gloster Meteor, but it was not until January 1957 that the squadron was equipped with the Hawker Hunter F6. However, this was only a temporary measure as No.63 was disbanded on 30 October 1958.

In 1963 No.63 became a shadow squadron for the day fighter combat school, based at Binbrook, flying Hunter F6s, but once again it was disbanded in January 1966. The instructors and equipment were transferred to No.229 OCU, then at Chivenor.

The unit moved to Brawdy in August 1974 to become a tactical weapons unit. The Hunters were replaced by BAe Hawks in 1979, and in August 1980 returned to Chivenor as a nucleus of No.2 TWU.

The squadron badge shows a forepart of an arm grasping a battle-axe. The motto translates to 'Follow us to the enemy'.

No.79 Squadron, No.229 OCU, No.1 Tactical Weapon Unit

No.79 Squadron was formed at Gosport on 1 August 1917, but moved within a week to Beaulieu, providing advance training on Sopwith Dolphin.

The squadron moved to France on 20 February 1918 and was utilised for ground attack, where it suffered a high rate of casualties. After the war it formed part of the occupation army based in Germany, where it was disbanded on 15 July 1919.

No.79 Squadron was reformed at Biggin Hill on 22 March 1937, and equipped with Gloster Gauntlets, to become part of the air defence of Greater London. In November 1938 the squadron was re-equipped with the Hawker Hurricane MkI, and was hurriedly sent to France in May 1940. Before returning to the UK the squadron had claimed twenty-five enemy aircraft destroyed in ten days. By August 1940 No.79 Squadron was heavily involved in the Battle of Britain, and by the end of the battle they had acquired seventy-six victories.

In March 1942 the unit moved overseas to India, with the brand new Hurricane MkII, armed with 20mm cannons, and were involved in reconnaissance and bomber escort duties and army co-operation. They were also used to escort Dakotas on supply drop missions. In May 1944 the squadron was re-equipped with the American Thunderbolt fighter-bombers.

With the cessation of hostilities, No.79 squadron was disbanded at Meikela, Burma, on 30 December 1945.

For the next few years the squadron remained dormant, but was reformed at Gutersloh in Germany in November 1951 as a fighter reconnaissance unit equipped with Gloster Meteor FR9s, which were later replaced by the Supermarine Swift FR5 in June 1955.

In January 1961 the squadron was disbanded once again, and its personnel and aircraft were absorbed into the now reformed No.4 Squadron.

In 1967 the squadron was reformed once again as the third shadow unit, and allocated to No.229 Operational Conversion Unit, based at Chivenor with Hawker Hunter FGA9s and FR10s, used for advance tactical reconnaissance training.

In September 1974 the OCU moved to RAF Brawdy and became Tactical Weapons Unit. The squadron was joined by four Jet Provost trainers, which provided refresher-flying training to the pilots. In mid-seventies the unit provided Hunter detachments at Gibraltar.

During the 1978 reorganisation Brawdy became No1 TWU with No79 retaining its shadow squadron status within the unit. The squadron Hawker Hunters was replaced by the BAe Hawk T1/1A in 1984.

In January 1992, due to a defence review, all flying training ceased at Brawdy, and TWU was disbanded. The last training flight was made on 28 August 1992 by ten Hawks belonging to Nos 79 and 234 Squadrons. It marked a sad day in the history of both squadrons, as in 1992 Nos 79 and 234 Squadrons celebrated their seventy-fifth anniversaries.

The squadron badge is a salamander salient with the motto 'Nil nobis obstare potest', translated to 'Nothing can stop us'.

No.234 Squadron, No.229 OCU, No.1 Tactical Weapons Unit

No.234 Squadron was formed in August 1918 from a RNAS flying boat unit based at Tresco with Curtiss H12s, Felixstowe F2As and F3 flying boats. Like most First World War squadrons, it was disbanded on 15 May 1919.

The squadron was reformed at RAF Leconfield on 30 October 1939, equipped with a collection of different types of Avro Tutors, Miles Magisters trainers, Bristol Blenheim 1Fs, Gloster Gauntlets and Fairey Battles. In March 1940 Spitfire Mk1s replaced the mixed collection, and the squadron left Yorkshire for St Eval in Cornwall, from where it took part in the Battle of Britain.

Between April 1942 and September 1943 the squadron was involved in convoy escorts, shipping reconnaissance duties and fighter sweeps over France. By now No.234 had been re-equipped with a later mark of Spitfire, and provided air cover for the Normandy landings.

In September 1944 the squadron was re-equipped yet again with the North American Mustangs, providing long-range escorts and patrols over Germany. In August 1945 the Mustangs were replaced by Spitfire Mk IXs and the jet-powered fighter, the Meteor F3, in February 1946, but was disbanded on 31 August to form No.245 Squadron.

No.234 was reformed on 1 August 1952 as part of 2 Tactical Air Force fighter unit at Oldenburg, Germany, with de Havilland Vampire Mk5 and 9s, converting to Canadair-built Sabres in June 1953.

The RAF acquired several hundred Sabres as a stopgap until the Hawker Hunter jet entered service in May 1956. The squadron was disbanded once again on 15 July 1957, to be reformed on 30 November 1958 at RAF Chivenor, as a shadow squadron of No.229 Operational Conversion Unit, equipped with Hawker Hunter F6 and FR9s.

Although the OCU was disbanded the squadron moved to RAF Brawdy in September 1974 to form a tactical weapons unit.

In 1978 the Hunters were gradually withdrawn from service and replaced by the British Aerospace Hawk T1, which became the mainstay of the TWU. On 26 February 1992 the squadron celebrated its seventy-fifth anniversary, a hollow celebration as the squadron was disbanded on 28 August 1992.

The squadron badge features a dragon rampant with flames coming from his mouth. The motto is 'Ignem mortemque despuimus', translated to 'We spit fire and death'.

Similar titles available from The History Press

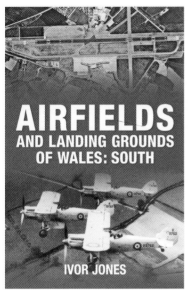

Airfields and Landing Grounds of Wales: South
Ivor Jones

The first in a three-volume series chronicling the location, history and fate of the many landing grounds, airfields and airports of Wales, this book focuses on the south.

Starting at the English border with Chepstow and finishing in Llandovery, Ivor Jones details such diverse histories as the meadows, parks and golf courses that were used as landing grounds by the United States Army's liaison aircraft during the Second World War, the RAF stations in the Vale of Glamorgan and the long forgotten civil aerodromes of the 1930s that served to give flight to the average man.

£16.99
978 0 7524 4273 0

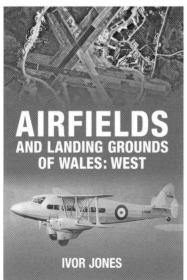

Airfields and Landing Grounds of Wales: West
Ivor Jones

This is the second book in Ivor Jones's three-volume series, *The Airfields and Landing Grounds of Wales*, and covers the west. The airfields and landing grounds in this area include RAF Fairwood Common, RAF Pembrey, Castle Martin, Ilford Haven fuel depot, RAF Dale, Picton Castle Camp cubstrip, RAF Haverfordwest, RAF St David's and RAF Aberporth.

Combining the history of the airfields with previously unpublished archive photographs, maps and aerial shots, this is a highly detailed and informative book.

£16.99
978 0 7524 4418 5

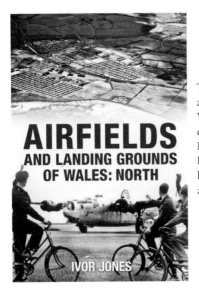

Airfields and Landing Grounds of Wales: North
Ivor Jones

The last in a three-volume series chronicling the location, history and fate of the many landing grounds, airfields and airports of Wales, this book focuses on the north. This informative book covers RAF Towyn, Broomhill, Hell's Mouth, RAF Valley, RAF Mona, cubstrip at Denbigh, RAF Sealand, RAF Poulton and RAF Wrexham, and comprises a mixture of informative text, history, anecdotes and maps, and a wealth of archive aerial shots and photographs.

£16.99
978 0 7524 4510 4

Visit our website and discover thousands of other History Press books.

www.thehistorypress.co.uk